Social Policy in Action

D1645620

by Joan L. M. Eyden

Senior Lecturer in Social Administration
University of Nottingham

LONDON
ROUTLEDGE & KEGAN PAUL
NEW YORK: HUMANITIES PRESS

First published 1969
by Routledge & Kegan Paul Ltd.
Broadway House, 68-74 Carter Lane
London, E.C.4

Printed in Great Britain by
Northumberland Press Limited,
Gateshead

SBN 7100 6402 0 (c)
SBN 7100 6404 7 (p)

the general rise in the standard of living and the diminution of economic inequality as strengthening the demand for the abolition of social inequality.

> These aspirations have in part been set by incorporating social rights in the status of citizenship and thus creating a universal right to real income which is not proportionate to the market values of the claimant. Class-abatement is still the aim of social rights but it has acquired a new meaning. It is no longer merely an attempt to abate the obvious nuisance of destitution in the lowest ranks of society. It has assumed the guise of action modifying the whole pattern of social inequality (T. H. Marshall, 1963).

This kind of debate will, no doubt, continue but both these references tend to under-emphasise those aspects of social policy which are concerned with the provision of communal facilities and with social action for the improvement of the conditions under which individuals live and work.

Conflicting aims and methods of social policy

For the purpose of this book social policy is taken as including those courses of action adopted by the government which relate to the social aspects of life, action which is deliberately designed and taken to improve the welfare of its citizens, either collectively or as individuals. Certain problems arise.

Implicit in certain policies may be values or ends which conflict either with each other or with values or ends already being promoted by existing laws, regulations or services. Thus the introduction of the 'wages stop' into the administration of national assistance was an attempt to reconcile two 'goods'. It has been held that it is a 'good thing' that the state should ensure that all its members have sufficient means to achieve a minimum standard of living expressed by the basic rate of national assistance current at the time. It has also been held that it is a 'good thing' for all able-bodied men to work to support themselves and their immediate dependants. The wages stop whereby the Board under the National Assistance (Determination of Need) Regulations, 1948, restricted the assistance payable to an unemployed person to ensure that his total income did not exceed the income he would have had if he were in full-time employment was introduced as a device to reconcile these two 'goods'. This restriction was the corollary of the provision in the Act which prevented the Board from supplementing the wages of persons working full-time.

The example of the wages stop has elements which we must pursue further. This administrative device, designed to reconcile two different policy aims, assumed that any man in full-time work was able to support himself and his dependants at a standard acceptable to himself and the rest of the community without any help additional to that provided for his fellow-workers; further, that unless his situation when unemployed was 'less eligible' than when he was in full-time work he was unlikely to seek and hold work. These implications are of a somewhat different order from those mentioned earlier as they are, in theory at least, based upon ascertainable *facts* not beliefs or values.

Any study of social policy must seek to differentiate between these elements, the values or ends implicit and explicit in any suggested course of action—values or ends which may reinforce one another, may be complementary or may be in conflict—and the factual knowledge which may be available from research in economics, psychology, sociology and other social sciences. In practice it is sometimes difficult to disentangle these elements. Our knowledge from the social sciences is only slowly accumulating and becoming available for use; moreover some problems which are theoretically capable of solution have not been

6

solved because of inadequate resources of research personnel, difficulties of method or inability on the part of the government, universities or the general public to recognise the help which may be obtained from such research. Consequently those responsible for making and implementing social policy are often forced to act in the light of the information available. This inadequacy of knowledge makes it particularly difficult to distinguish between differences in beliefs held because of genuine conflicts of value and those views held as 'informed opinions' based on partial knowledge or inspired guesses. It is unlikely that these difficulties will ever be completely resolved but increasing knowledge from the social sciences may help the policy-maker to come to decisions based on a greater understanding of the possible outcome of any particular course of action.

The traditional method of obtaining information upon which to base new developments in social policy has been through the appointment of *ad hoc* Commissions and departmental or inter-departmental committees of enquiry bringing together experts who can gather relevant information, obtain the opinions and views of interested parties and on this basis advise the government about the particular problem or field of concern under consideration. In March 1966 five Royal Commissions and thirty-eight specially appointed committees were inquiring into questions of public importance. Some services have permanent advisory committees at different levels of administration, often set up under statute, whose job it is to keep the Minister abreast of expert opinion, and one of the important functions of the higher civil service is to have available facts and information relevant to the department. The growth of statistical information about every area of life is an outstanding phenomenon of modern society although such information is not always available in the most useful form.

Problems of compulsion

How far, and in what circumstances should the individual
be compelled to undertake courses of action which the
government decides are for his own or other people's good?
We are compelled to be contributors to a social security
scheme to provide ourselves with some protection if illness or unemployment should strike, although we are not
compelled to accept benefit. Children are compelled to go
to school between the ages of five and fifteen unless alternative arrangements are made for their education deemed
satisfactory by the local education authority. In certain
circumstances we can be compelled to receive care and
treatment for mental disorder but not for cancer; we can
be forced to enter an isolation hospital if we have contact
with smallpox but not if we are ill with influenza. At one
time we could be compelled to be vaccinated against smallpox but not immunised against diphtheria.

As already mentioned, most social policy is the result
of a compromise between conflicting interests, an attempt
to balance the right to freedom of action of individuals or
groups with the welfare of others. No clear answer can be
given to the question—when should an individual or group
be compelled to some action or to receive care or treatment in his own or others interests against his express
wish? In the case of mental illness this problem is one
which has caused controversy and concern for many years.
After much discussion the nineteenth century came down
on the side of safeguarding the liberty of the individual
at the expense of inhibiting the early seeking of hospital
care by an elaborate process of legal certification before
a 'lunatic' could be admitted to an asylum without his
consent. The Mental Health Act, 1959, introduced a new
procedure which amounted to a new principle, a departure
from established policy: a patient suffering from mental
disorder can be compulsorily admitted to hospital for

observation or treatment without the intervention of any judicial authority but at the request of the relative or an officer of the local authority on medical recommendation. Facilities for early discharge and the right of appeal to a Mental Health Review Tribunal are considered to be sufficient safeguards against wrongful detention. In other circumstances resort to the Courts is still necessary as in the case of the removal of a child from the care of its parents without their consent if he is deemed to be in need of care, protection or control. A similar procedure is necessary for the removal for care and attention of a person suffering from grave chronic disease or, being aged, infirm or physically handicapped is living in insanitary conditions, in his own interest under Section 47 of the National Assistance Act, 1948. It is perhaps noteworthy that in 1953 only 250 and in 1959 only 165 people were so dealt with. The considerable amount of discussion which followed the publication of the White Paper *The Child, the Family and the Young Offender*, with its suggestion of Family Councils to replace the jurisdiction of the Juvenile Courts in certain circumstances, is another example of the ambivalent feelings of society about the whole question of compulsion in the alleged interests of the individuals concerned.

In a large complex society such as ours, regulation by government action and the due processes of law is a very important aspect of social control yet it is only part of the total pressures upon the individual.

Man is a social animal in that he cannot satisfy his needs except in relation with his fellows. Our needs force us to make claims upon others, and force us to recognise also that others must make the same claims upon us. And so, at the very heart of human nature and human conduct there is mutuality and reciprocity (Fletcher, 1965).

This mutuality and reciprocity has been a potent force in shaping social policy.

2

Implementing social policy

Regulation, subsidy and the social services

Policy directed towards the welfare of citizens may take
many forms and the methods used to implement them may
equally be extremely varied. Some of the earliest legislation of this kind was concerned with the environmental
conditions under which people have lived. Thus, in the
thirteenth century, charter boroughs dealt with nuisances
under bye-laws; some of these as early as 1298 dealt with
the cleansing of streets and keeping pigs in houses. In 1388
the first Sanitary Act was an attempt to abate nuisances
in their relation to disease. But it was only with the increasing complexity of urbanised and industrialised society
that the importance of environmental legislation was
recognised, forming one of the earliest and most extensive
exceptions to the *laissez-faire* policy of the nineteenth century. Edwin Chadwick's report in 1842 *Sanitary Conditions
of the Labouring Population of Great Britain* and the report
two years later of a Royal Commission on the health of
towns brought to light the conditions under which many
people were living. The connection between ill-health,
poverty and insanitary environmental factors was demon-

strated with telling effect and led to the beginning of a long series of Public Health Acts which have gradually helped to reduce the death-rate from 22·5 per thousand population per annum in the period 1861-70 to 11·7 in 1966.

Much social policy is concerned with the attempt to protect those who are thought to be the weaker members of society, children, young people, women, mental defectives or those who are particularly exposed to hazards such as those employed in dangerous trades. Thus the promoters of early factory legislation found that an appeal to humanity was most easily made about children and the first decisive steps to safeguard their health and well-being were taken in 1833 and 1847 during the period which is usually considered as obsessed by the doctrine of *laissez-faire*. The revelation of the appalling conditions of female and child labour in coal-mines led to the Mines Act, 1842 which forbade the employment underground of women and of children under ten years. By an Act of 1850 adult males were also protected by a Mines Inspectorate, and step by step the provision of safety precautions in the mines became the concern of the state. Similarly by a series of statutes from 1808 to 1845 a measure of public responsibility was accepted for the care of patients suffering from mental illness.

Legislation embodying this protective type of social policy is often negative in character; it prohibits certain forms of behaviour or restricts the action of individuals or groups in some defined way. Thus public water supplies may not be polluted; inhabited dwellings have to comply with certain regulations; employers must provide amenities for their staff; the employment of children is severely restricted; the hours which women may work are regulated; in certain circumstances the mentally ill may be detained in hospital for their own and other people's safety and welfare.

In contrast to this approach, social policy may be implemented by the encouragement of personal consumption of certain goods or the development of private enterprise along certain lines or in particular places. Two ways in which this more positive approach is seen are the use made of the fiscal system as an instrument of public policy, and the giving of direct or indirect subsidies. Since the introduction of progressive taxation in 1907 the fiscal system has been used to assist a taxpayer to meet his family responsibilities. Firms may be attracted to new towns or development areas by financial inducements on social as well as economic grounds. Better nutrition among the young is encouraged by the provision of free or cheap welfare foods and by subsidising school meals. Similarly, heavy taxation can be used as a disincentive to the consumption of articles which are thought to be injurious. In many instances it is difficult to determine the primary aim of some actions, so closely are social and economic factors involved, as in the duty on tobacco.

Increasingly, however, the State has been concerned with the promotion of the welfare of its citizens by more direct means and has taken responsibility for providing services to meet certain needs of individuals and groups.

The earliest example of public provision for those in need was the responsibility placed on the parishes to relieve their own destitute by the series of statutes in the sixteenth century which culminated in the Poor Law in 1601. This Act remained the basis of public provision for the poor until its final abolition—after much amendment —in 1948. However, the statutory social services developed from cautious, hesitant and sometimes seemingly accidental beginnings in the latter years of the nineteenth century into the complex of public provision which we call today the Welfare State. The pioneer experiments of philanthropists and of working-class organisations were used as prototypes for increasing government intervention. After the National Insurance Act of 1911 some measure of security in sickness, unemployment, and later, in old age, widowhood and orphanhood was provided on an insurance basis; financial assistance for old people, the blind, the chronically unemployed and their families was given outside the Poor Law while the Poor Law itself, reformed and liberalised and gradually dispelling the impression that those in receipt of assistance from public funds were second-class citizens, developed into a residual service underpinning more specialised provision. The maternal and child welfare service, the school health service and particularly the provision of education itself, all contributed to the growing interest and involvement of the state in the welfare of its citizens and particularly of its younger members.

Thus have grown up the services concerned with the needs of individuals and groups. One of the earliest uses of the term 'public social service' was in connection with the first return of expenditure under certain Acts of Parliament which provided 'direct beneficiary assistance'—a return made at the request of an M.P., Mr. Drage in 1913. This return included money spent on unemployed and health insurance, education, public health and poor relief. Lord Eustace Percy, in *Government in Transition* (1934), suggested that what people usually thought of as social services were those 'which are designed more directly to benefit the citizen as an individual'. The P.E.P. Report of 1937 on the British Social Services, defined them as those 'which have as their object the enhancement of the personal welfare of individual citizens'. These descriptions would appear to suggest that social services are benevolent in intention and that they are designed to benefit people directly or individually, although not all writers are agreed that social services necessarily have this individual personal element. Thus Sir George Newman in *The English Social Services* includes libraries, museums, and even communications and transport. The P.E.P. Broadsheet *Planning* (No. 354 in 1953) argued that 'Public water and sewage services, although socially provided, are normally regarded as environmental or physical services and not services personal to the family or individual. Public parks, libraries and museums are seen primarily as local amenities rather than personal welfare services, although the distinction is not sharp.'

Universality and social rights

One of the fundamental changes which has taken place during the past half-century is the way in which measures originally conceived as applying to a small minority of persons in particular need, specially vulnerable or with particular claims on the compassion of others, have been extended to cover all classes in the community. Obvious examples are the extension of national insurance from those manual workers under a contract of service and other employed persons of small income, to all of working age; of the provision of a general practitioner service for every member of the community; the availability of allowances to all families containing more than one dependent child without test of income and the powers given to local authorities to build houses without these being limited to occupancy by 'the working classes'. The provision of school dinners began as a method of preventing the benefits of state education from being wasted on children who were too hungry and undernourished to use the opportunities they were being given but these are now available to all schoolchildren and in 1965 more than 65% of children in England and Wales made use of them.

Moreover social policy has become increasingly concerned with the personal problems and difficulties of individuals as, for instance, with marital relationships, with the quality of care of parents for their children, with social

14

life in new housing areas and in the relationships between management and workers.

The greater knowledge and understanding of some of the problems which have come from this interest and concern has in its turn led to renewed attempts to create more favourable living and working conditions. Thus has arisen a new concept of social planning, an attempt to develop a healthy and less stressful environment in a more comprehensive and positive way than the efforts to control the physical environment associated with the public health and factory Acts of the nineteenth century onwards. Examples of this kind of social policy are seen in the planning of the new towns where the urgent necessity of providing new housing and working communities for the overspill of the heavily populated areas of the country has been used to try out some exciting experiments of social planning.

These three developments—the greater universality of social provision, the increased concern of the state with the personal life of its citizens, and an acceptance of a new concept of social planning—have had a profound effect on the machinery of government and methods of administration. They have meant a great increase in the number and variety of the organs of government and a new concept of the relationship between public agencies and the public served. In some instances new departments or boards have been created with national, regional or local responsibilities. Perhaps more usually, central or local government departments have been given further powers extending the range of existing functions. Occasionally voluntary organisations have been used as agents or have been encouraged to work in close partnership with statutory services. The result is a complex pattern of administrative organisations which would seem to indicate by their variety that different types of organisation are more appropriate for different categories of social action.

In commenting on a series of case studies describing and analysing the evolution of the services provided by certain voluntary and public organisations Donnison states that it is possible to analyse administration by the use of the three concepts—task, process and organisation. 'Once the task has been specified it is possible to discover the processes that play a part in its accomplishment, and once the process has been traced it becomes possible to abstract the pattern of roles, rules and relationships which constitutes the administrative organisation for this work' (Donnison, 1965). This suggests that tasks having similar characteristics and thus demanding some similarity of administrative process should result in the establishment of organisations having like structural patterns or even in the same organisation undertaking a number of similar kinds of task. For instance it could be expected that the task of providing financial help during periods of unemployment on an insurance basis would result in administrative processes and organisation very similar to that carrying out the task of providing financial help during periods of illness or during retirement from work. Historically the social insurance schemes providing for these contingencies before the coming into force of the National Insurance Act, 1946 had a number of similar features but also many that were quite unlike. The administrative integration of these schemes was one of the achievements of this Act. Similar integration in other fields of social action has not necessarily been achieved, however, and an examination of the organisations which have evolved to implement the different aspects of social policy shows the complexity of provision and process, and in places an administrative specialisation which it is difficult to justify on any but historical grounds.

In an examination of such organisations different methods of categorisation may be used. They may be grouped according to the degree of statutory responsibility, the area of action, the complexity of function, the prime beneficiary, etc. In the remainder of this chapter and in succeeding ones, efforts will be made to explore some of the significance of categories based on these characteristics.

Voluntary and statutory organisations

A classification of organisations often made in studying social action is into those which are *statutory*—based on legislation which gives permissive or mandatory powers to the government to create organs to carry out certain policies, and those which are *voluntary* or *private*—initiated and governed by their members. This distinction based on mode of birth and government can have profound repercussions on the character and method of operation of the organisation. Thus statutory bodies are accountable to the public and are largely financed by funds raised by taxation or other forms of compulsory levy on citizens, whereas voluntary organisations are dependent on the goodwill of private citizens or corporate bodies and, within the limits set by the law in order to prevent fraud and abuse of funds, are accountable only to their governing body according to the particular constitution of the organisation.

Voluntary organisations have traditionally been pioneers, identifying needs, experimenting with methods of meeting these needs, and educating public opinion. It is often stated that such organisations are flexible, able to undertake new work or use new methods without seeking fresh statutory powers and are able to concern themselves with minority causes in a way which would be difficult for government bodies with their strict rules of public accountability. Statutory organisations have often made use of the special experience of voluntary societies for a time before providing a direct comprehensive service themselves. An illustration of this was the use made of Friendly Societies as approved agents in the administration of the first national health insurance scheme and of voluntary hospitals to provide the Emergency Hospital Service during the 1939-45 War.

Still common are the arrangements which many local authorities make with voluntary organisations for the welfare of the blind or other handicapped persons to provide certain services on their behalf under the National Assistance Acts, 1948 and 1962, or with district nursing associations to provide home nursing under the National Health Service Act, 1946. It is noticeable, however, that a number of these arrangements are coming to an end as local authorities gain more experience in these fields of public action and resolve to establish their own direct service which can then be more closely integrated with other personal services.

Rapidly changing conditions throw up new needs, cause new stresses and lead to fresh pioneer ventures on the part of the voluntary organisations, both old and new. It is a study in itself to trace the way in which many old-established bodies are prepared to change and adapt to modern demands; others unfortunately linger on providing an inefficient and overlapping service, while yet others quietly go out of business. The existence of so many voluntary organisations working often in close partnership with central and local government bodies indicates that there are other functions for such organisations less temporary than the purely pioneer one. The use made by local authorities of special schools and children's homes run by voluntary bodies indicates that these have an important role in providing for the very special needs of small groups, as for children with multiple handicaps, or for minority groups on religious or similar grounds. They may provide services in fields where there is considerable public controversy as in family planning. An interesting development has been the very close partnership which exists

18

between voluntary organisations and local authorities in the Youth Service which provides for a wide variety of leisure-time activities, giving an essential freedom of choice to the individual in this field.

Nevertheless, while close co-operation between statutory and voluntary bodies in the field of social action is important, the essential contribution which the latter can make is in their ability to take independent action. Too great a dependence on government help, whether in money or expertise, can affect their role as critics of state action or inaction, and as pressure groups to get more and better public provision in their particular field of concern. The dialogue between statutory and voluntary organisation in the field of public action can and should be a fruitful one.

Most of our major social services illustrate the way in which needs met in a partial, piecemeal way by voluntary initiative have been gradually recognised as being the concern of the whole community and incorporated into the general body of public services. Moreover as our society has become increasingly complex, more highly industrialised and urbanised, so services which in the first place were thought of as being needed only by the specially unfortunate and underprivileged can be used with advantage by all citizens. When this situation arises such services are more appropriately provided by the state. The most outstanding example of this is the National Health Service. The necessities of war demanded comprehensive provision, efficiently organised to make the best use of scarce resources; the Emergency Medical Service improvised such a service based on existing provision and paved the way for the development of a more permanent peace-time organisation. Public opinion, fired by the Beveridge Report, was favourable to the replacement of the chaotic pre-war provision by a comprehensive service and thus under the terms of the National Health Service Act, 1946, the Minister of Health was given the duty 'to promote the establishment in England and Wales of a comprehensive health service designed to secure improvement in the physical and mental health of the people'. The Government, as the representatives of the community, thus assumed the clear duty of responsibility for meeting the health needs of the nation and the National Health Service is used by all classes of society. Thus the P.E.P. Report, *Family Needs and the Social Services* (1961) found that 99% of all families in their sample had made some use of this service during the period under review.

The view that the development of our mid-twentieth-century statutory services—health, education, insurance, social assistance—is one manifestation of a process which has been going on for several centuries to re-establish citizen rights has already been noted. Social policy aimed at greater social justice, at creating conditions which seek to ensure a greater degree of equality of opportunity, at securing social rights inevitably means a great increase in statutory as opposed to voluntary provision to meet need.

3

Administrative responsibility and complexity of function

Both statutory and voluntary organisations implementing social policy may differ considerably in the internal complexity of their administrative structure and in limitation of their responsibilities either geographically or functionally. In the case of statutory provision this is complicated by the existence of a tradition of responsible local authorities and the problems of relationship between central and local government.

National, regional and local organisations

Until recently, by far the greatest use has been made in both voluntary and statutory services of central and local units of administration, but the possibility of regional organisations, especially in the field of planning, is being explored with new interest.

A development in the last half-century has been the growth in size and complexity of organisation of many voluntary bodies as they have tried to become more complete in coverage. Sometimes the pattern is one of a national organisation with a central office and regional or local branches with more or less independence. Sometimes the central organisation affiliates semi-autonomous local bodies which fulfil certain conditions; or yet again fully independent local bodies come together periodically in a standing conference for the interchange of information and experience or to formulate a common policy. Thus the Red Cross, the National Society for the Prevention of Cruelty to Children, the National Association of Boys' Clubs all show different organisational patterns. The tensions that can arise from time to time in almost any service between national, regional and local interests are illustrated in M. Rooff's discussion of voluntary effort in welfare work for the blind (Rooff, 1957).

In the statutory field the division between services organised nationally and those provided by local bodies often seems to have only historical justification. Fear and dislike of central government control tended to limit the functions of the Crown and ministers to those activities essential for the safety and peace of the realm. However, during the last hundred years the outstanding developments in the field of public administration have been the growing power of the central government, largely exercised through powerful departments headed by a Minister of the Crown and run by an efficient, impartial and loyal civil service; and the enlargement of the effective unit of local government—from parish to district council to county council and in some instances to national body. These changes have been necessary to carry out the work of government in a highly complex, industrialised society.

The central departments are responsible for the more detailed development of policy laid down by Parliament and its implementation. Within broadly defined areas of government the functions of the departments are often extremely diverse. The Ministry of Health, created in 1919, had, until 1951, additional responsibility for the general oversight of local government. The Ministry now has the duty of seeing that a comprehensive health service

is provided for all citizens who wish to use it and of ensuring that public health legislation is effective. It has
differing degrees of responsibility for the work of Regional
Hospital Boards, Boards of Governors of teaching hospitals
and Executive Councils, all of whose members are appointed, and for the elected local health authorities. One
of the few services provided directly by the Ministry of
Health is the maintenance and administration of the
'special' hospitals such as those providing maximum
security for certain mentally disordered patients.

The responsibility of the Ministry of Education, which
replaced the old Board of Education in 1944, was almost
entirely concerned with the oversight of the education service provided by local authorities—including nursery,
primary, secondary and special schools, colleges of further
education, various ancillary education services, youth
clubs and community centres. In 1964 it was renamed the
Department of Education and Science and has also become
responsible for the encouragement of scientific research
and for the needs of universities. The Home Office (which
dates back to 1782) and the Ministry of Housing and Local
Government (created in 1951) are examples of government
departments with a great variety of functions, which are
also primarily concerned with the general oversight of
local authority and other services. Since the demise of the
Prison Commission in 1964, the Home Office in addition
to its primary duty of maintaining the Queen's Peace has
direct responsibility for the provision and administration
of all prisons and borstals. Much of the work of the departments already mentioned is carried out centrally, although
regional offices are often maintained to facilitate contact
with local authorities and, where appropriate, with the
general public.

The Ministry of Labour and the Ministry of Social
Security are, however, primarily concerned with the provision of direct services to the public and not with the

oversight of local authorities. The Ministry of Labour, through its regional offices and nation-wide network of employment exchanges, provides comprehensive coverage —even to the extent of mobile interviewing units where necessary—in order to ensure that those who are unemployed, or about to become so, are placed in appropriate jobs with the minimum of delay. The work of the Ministry has been brought into particular prominence of recent years owing to the need for the redeployment of labour due to changes in demand and in technological processes. The Ministry of Social Security, which replaced the Ministry of Pensions and National Insurance in 1966, also maintains a regional and local administrative structure although much of its activity is centred on its huge central record office. Many queries about contributions and benefits have to be sorted out locally by personal interview.

The Board of Trade, the Commissioners of Inland Revenue and other central government bodies all have a part to play in the implementation of social policy. The first is responsible, among many other duties, for measures concerning the location of industry, and thus is an important instrument in ensuring the redevelopment of areas of underemployment and a more socially desirable distribution of industry. The important role which the Commissioners of Inland Revenue play in making certain aspects of social policy effective through the fiscal system has already been noted.

Responsibility for local government is divided mainly between county councils and the minor authorities—urban and rural district councils and borough councils; parish councils now have very little power. Most cities are county boroughs combining the duties and powers of both county and borough councils in one single authority. County councils were established by the Local Government Act, 1888, and urban and rural district councils by that of 1894. Many of the boroughs were of ancient origin and

24

were reformed by the Municipal Corporations Act, 1835.

The minor authorities, that is the boroughs and the rural and urban district councils, are responsible for housing, the provision of a number of amenity services, and traditional duties concerned with sanitation and other matters of environmental health. County councils are responsible for education, the fire service, town and country planning and a number of services concerned with personal health and welfare. There has been a tendency for new local services to be given to the major authorities —as the care of deprived children in 1948—and for some developing services to be transferred, as with the provision of maternal and child welfare and similar domiciliary services which became the responsibility of the county and county borough councils under the National Health Service Act, 1946. However, since the Local Government Act, 1958, some of the larger borough and district councils have had delegated responsibility for certain personal health and welfare services.

The former two-tier system in the administrative county of London, the London County Council and the metropolitan boroughs, was replaced under the London Government Act, 1963, by a number of new boroughs with most of the powers and duties of county boroughs although education remains for a period with an Inner London Education Authority covering the same area as the old London County Council; a new Greater London Council has responsibility for transport, planning and certain other functions for which a large area is more appropriate.

Although they are elected bodies, the local authorities form part of the general administrative hierarchy. They are subject to much central control and in some respects have become virtually organs of the central government. As a result of this development it may be asked whether the local authorities serve any useful function. Where there is need for uniformity of administration over the country as a whole and where the citizen has a right to a high level of service wherever he may live, it is suggested that the central government should become directly responsible for the running of services. Thus, in education, which is already substantially subsidised by the Exchequer and yet is still a heavy charge on local rates, there has been great variation in the number of grammar school places available for children of allegedly equal ability in different local education authorities. This is held to result in some children being less privileged than their peers in other areas and to make nonsense of the idea of the right to education according to age, aptitude and ability. In spite of central government control, local authorities have considerable initiative and can act in accordance with local opinion, both in education and in other matters affecting the citizen. The example of the controversy over the development of comprehensive, secondary education—a development advocated by the Labour Government in order to promote a greater equality of opportunity—shows the way in which local authorities are able to prevent or at least to delay the implementation of social policy adopted at national level.

The existence of permissive legislation, the powers of local authorities to make bye-laws in certain circumstances and the fact that they can obtain special powers by local Acts of Parliament, all mean that there may be considerable divergence in the services and controls in different local areas. These variations do not always seem to reflect real differences in local needs or problems. Thus in 1964 Blackpool, Staffordshire and County Durham each provided between eight and nine places in residential homes for persons aged sixty-five and over, per 1,000 of that age group, whereas Wolverhampton provided 20·7, Shropshire 20·0 and figures for Preston, Middlesbrough and Barnsley were 30·1, 32 and 33 respectively.

It is often considered that the personal social services

are most appropriately provided by local authorities. The Royal Commission on Local Government in Greater London reporting in 1960 was convinced that such services should be provided by an elected local authority and preferably by a small authority responsible for a population between 100,000 and 200,000.

> Our general view of the personal health, welfare and children's services is that since they deal mainly with the lives of people living in their own homes, they should be organised in as small units as is consistent with efficiency. The various services should operate whenever possible from one council building, and there should be a conscious effort to achieve good team work between the officers concerned. They should not be mere voices on the telephone or signatures of letters to each other, but the man or woman down the corridor.

Although the recommendations of the Royal Commission were mostly accepted by the Government, the suggested size of the new local authority was modified so that the London boroughs created by the Act of 1963 vary in size from Kingston-on-Thames (146,470) to Lambeth (339,560).

Some critics have challenged the views of the members of the Royal Commission and suggest that there is little evidence to support the contention that the personal social services are necessarily provided more efficiently by a locally elected body or that the area of administration should be as small as possible. The very fact that the social services are providing increasingly personal and individual forms of help necessitating the employment of a variety of professional people may make local control by elected councillors inappropriate. Too small a unit of administration may mean an inefficient deployment of scarce specialised resources, militate against the recruitment of staff of the highest calibre and cause increasing financial difficul-

27

ties in the poorer areas where the demand for such personal services is likely to be heaviest. Local responsibility for local residents in distress may have been appropriate when the Elizabethan Poor Law was developed or when the Act of Settlement was passed, but may be totally unsuitable for our highly mobile society.

The growing interest in the development of regional units of administration arises because regionalism is seen as a possible solution to three distinct but related problems—the reform of local government which at present is often bedevilled by the existence of many small financially weak authorities and by an unreal distinction between town and country, regional development and planning primarily concerned with land use, and regional decentralisation of central government administration as a means to the improvement of such administration and to a closer liaison with local interests and groups. Many civil servants are already employed in regional organisations of their departments, particularly in the ministries responsible for direct services to the public.

Ad hoc *and multi-purpose organisations*

Another possible type of classification is based on the complexity of the organisation chosen to carry out aspects of social policy. The social reforms of the nineteenth century show a number of examples of the establishment of new administrative bodies specially designed to implement new policy on an *ad hoc* basis. The elected local Boards of Guardians for the administration of the Poor Law in the unions of parishes created under the Poor Law Amendment Act, 1834, the local Boards of Health under the Public Health Act, 1848 and the School Boards established under the Education Act, 1870, are all illustrations of the way in which new experimental and specialist authorities had to be created owing to the absence or in-
28

adequacy of existing local bodies. The semi-independent central board was also used extensively in connection with the mid-nineteenth-century social reforms as in the creation of the General Board of Health, the Charity Commission, the Lunacy Commission and many others. The key minister for co-ordinating the new departments of central control was the Home Secretary, but his jurisdiction was loose and ill-defined, and as David Roberts (1960) points out, 'The Victorians' experiments in semi-dependent, non-political boards reflected their fear that administrative decision would be made the handmaid of party bias or be caught in the maelstrom of factional politics.' In 1871 the Local Government Board replaced some of these *ad hoc* central bodies. Others, reorganised and with new powers, lasted for many years, as for instance the Lunacy and Prison Commissions.

With the reform and reorganisation of local government which began with the Municipal Corporation Act, 1833, and was completed by the Local Government Acts, 1888 and 1894, most of the local *ad hoc* bodies were abolished and their functions absorbed into new multi-purpose authorities. The School Boards survived until 1902 and the Board of Guardians until 1929.

In spite of a trend towards multi-purpose authorities the twentieth century has seen the emergence of new specialist bodies fashioned to meet particular needs. An outstanding example was the creation of the Unemployment Assistance Board under the Unemployment Act, 1934—an attempt to place responsibility for giving financial help to the chronically unemployed and their families on a semi-independent non-political body, after the bitterness caused in some areas by the implementation of the household means test by Local Public Assistance Committees. In 1941 the Board was replaced by the Assistance Board with wider powers and this in turn was abolished with the setting up of the National Assistance Board by the National Assistance Act,

29

1948. Although the duties of the National Assistance Board were absorbed by the Ministry of Social Security in 1966, the setting up of a Supplementary Benefits Commission with powers to determine supplementary help to those in need perpetuates the use of an *ad hoc* corporate body.

The National Health Service Act made provision for the establishment of Regional Hospital Boards, Hospital Management Committees and Local Executive Councils. They are appointed, not elected, bodies broadly representative of local authorities and of professional and consumer interests in the area. They provide for a degree of local independence combined with central control. A similar interesting example of *ad hoc* bodies designed especially for the carrying out of post-war social policy are the New Town development corporations. The decision embodied in the New Towns Act, 1946 to provide additional centres for the growing population required machinery which could undertake the planning and establishment of these new urban areas.

Thus the *ad hoc* public corporation is a useful organ for implementation of government policy in certain conditions and Wade (1961) comments, 'It has a legal existence of its own, and can be given statutory duties and powers which fall outside the normal organisation of the service of the Crown. It offers scope for many kinds of government experiment, under which central control, local control and total independence can be blended in any desired proportions.' Corporations which form part of the administrative structure of social services are usually more closely controlled by their ministers than are corporations which manage industrial undertakings producing revenue such as the nationalised industries. Although responsible ministers can be called to account in Parliament in so far as they have exercised or failed to exercise their statutory powers of control, in practice the distinction between 'broad policy' and 'day-to-day administration' is often not too clear.

In spite of the usefulness of these types of *ad hoc* bodies most social policy is implemented through the various ministries and through the elected local authorities. The central government departments, headed by a Minister and staffed by civil servants, are responsible for broadly defined areas of administration but within these areas their functions are often extremely diverse. This inevitably means that each ministry is divided into many different sections, posing problems of co-ordination and co-operation.

Locally the development of multi-purpose authorities has been very evident particularly in those cities and towns of county borough status which are responsible for all local government functions. The increase in the number and scope of the services has meant a development of specialised departments and sub-departments. In some instances the administrative organisation used to implement a particular legislative provision is dictated by the Act itself or by regulation made under the Act. In others, particularly where permissive rather than mandatory powers are concerned, the local authority is free to decide the means whereby the service will be provided.

In theory, but not always in practice, the great advantage of multi-functional organisations is the greater ease whereby both policy and administration can be co-ordinated, leading to economies of financial and man-power resources and providing a more comprehensive and effective service to the citizen. At local government level the councils of the counties and county boroughs and their clerks are responsible for the overall co-ordination of the work of the various specialist committees and their departments. From the citizen's point of view it is less easy for an authority to disclaim responsibility for providing assistance in marginal cases of need if the disputed area of help lies between two departments of the same authority. Human need does not always fit neatly into administrative pigeon-holes. Thus it is argued that it is more difficult to meet the problems of homelessness in county areas where the housing authority is the district council, but the authority responsible for providing temporary accommodation is the county council, than in areas where the county borough is the all-purpose authority. Or again, disputes between hospital management committees and local authority welfare committees over responsibility for the infirm elderly are not uncommon.

Clarification of the function of the various departments or organisations involved and the definition of the roles of the workers are important aids to good co-operation. However, the development of services providing personal help to individuals means that it is more and more difficult to spell out eligibility requirements for service, or to define with any precision the boundaries of responsibility of the specialist department or worker; this may lead to apparent overlapping of function or gaps in provision. These difficulties may be resolved more easily within multi-functional organisations than between *ad hoc* bodies, and it is perhaps important, in deciding which kind of body is most appropriate in any particular instance, to give consideration to the extent to which clarity of function can be achieved.

The growth of personal services within multi-functional authorities can give rise to problems between the authority and the citizens it serves. Thus the local authority may be landlord, enforcer of school attendance, and provider of a casework service to the same family. It can arise that the social worker employed by one department of the authority may be required to give help of a highly personal kind with problems to which the authority itself may be a party.

A further difficulty is that with changing concepts of the role of the state in meeting personal needs and with the availability of greater knowledge and skill, developments take place in the operation of the services which amount to what is in effect a new function or a consider-

32

able enlargement of an existing one. Such a development may impinge upon the work already done by other departments or organisations, leading to confusion, misunderstandings and inefficient use of resources, until the situation is again clarified by administrative reorganisation and statutory changes. An interesting example of this is seen in the evolution of the child care service. Until the Children and Young Persons Act, 1963, there was considerable difference of opinion as to whether children's committees had the power to work with families to prevent children having to come into care, although in practice many authorities found themselves undertaking an increasing amount of such work. Section 1 of the 1963 Act gave additional duties to the local authorities to provide such a preventive service and the children's committees are primarily responsible. This development inevitably affects much of the personal work done by other departments of the local authorities, health, education, welfare and housing, as well as voluntary organisations such as the N.S.P.C.C. and Family Welfare Committees. Thus Section 1, while clarifying the powers of the local authorities, has added to the confusion concerning the division of responsibility within the local authorities and also between them and a number of other bodies. The growth of professional social work, the emphasis on a preventive approach and the increasing realisation of the importance of the family unit has led to the recognition that the whole area of the personal social services needs reorganisation and to the setting up of an inter-departmental committee by the Government in 1966 to study these services in England and Wales and to advise on any changes deemed necessary.

One difficulty which is likely to be found in the planning and operation of multi-functional bodies is that the optimum size of the organisation required for different purposes may vary. In the Acton Society Trust's study of regionalism (1964) it is pointed out that one of the argu-

33

ments against all-purpose regionalism under (perhaps) elected regional councils is that it is impossible to find one area which is technically suited to all services requiring large-scale administration. Each service needs to be assessed in terms of optimum area and/or population before a redefinition of areas is carried out. This is why a number of committees, both official and non-official, set up to consider specific aspects of government policy and administration have tended to reinforce the *ad hoc* 'special agency' concept whether the subject has been physical planning, the control of water resources, the location of industry or the reorganisation of the health service or of higher education. The proliferation of such *ad hoc* bodies however raises the question of democratic control. If regionalism grows, power would pass from the local authorities to independent appointed boards. At the same time the greater devolution by government departments to regional offices which has been advocated by some writers to avoid overmuch control or dictation in local affairs by the central government, would place more power in the hands of regional controllers.

The idea that there should be an elected council with responsibility for a large range of services over a wide area rather than a number of *ad hoc* authorities—a new version of the multi-functional body—will no doubt be taken into consideration in any future reorganisation of local government. The size of the areas chosen for such councils will inevitably have to be a compromise solution to the problem posed above, that different services appear to need different size population or land area for their optimum efficient organisation. Such bodies may provide a more effective means of co-ordinating both the planning and administration of services than *ad hoc* councils: they will however require a complex pattern of administrative organisation, and chief officers of high calibre and wide outlook.

34

4

Social policy and the concept of 'prime beneficiary'

An interesting basis for an analysis of organisations is suggested by Blau and Scott (1963) who have sought to use the concept of 'prime beneficiary'. They suggest that it is possible to distinguish four types of formal organisation by considering who chiefly benefits.

> Four types of organisations result from the application of our *cui bono* criterion: (1) 'mutual benefit associations', where the prime beneficiary is the membership; (2) 'business concerns', where the owners are prime beneficiary; (3) 'service organisations', where the client group is the prime beneficiary; and (4) 'commonweal organisations', where the prime beneficiary is the public-at-large.

Although they recognise that in the case of government departments the public is also the owner *and* prime beneficiary there are such major differences separating the two types—public organisations and privately owned ones—that they consider that no useful purpose is served by combining them into a single type.

In this chapter we shall be applying the *cui bono* principle to those organisations used for the implementation of social policy, and borrowing for our purposes this classification into four types of organisation. In fact these categories are not always easy to distinguish in practice, and a number of the organisational and administrative problems which arise in implementing social policy are to be found in those organisations, such as nationalised industries, which do not appear to fall neatly into this grouping. A casual study might lead us to expect that the categories of organisation with which we would be most concerned here would be those which seek to serve the 'client' public and those concerned with the 'Commonweal'. But as we have discussed already, successive governments have sought to influence both directly and indirectly mutual benefit associations and business concerns in the interests of the 'public-at-large' or of a particular group in the community.

Mutual-benefit associations

Organisations set up to promote the well-being of their members can be of many kinds. Trade unions, co-operative societies, friendly societies and social clubs are all examples. Although some may be considered as making a limited contribution to society, the influence of others has been of considerable importance in the development of the Welfare State. The 'self-help' or mutual-aid movements of the nineteenth century, of which the trade unions and friendly societies were important examples, not only helped to raise the standard of living of their members at a time of rapid social change and gave valuable training in democratic methods of government but also played a part in forming the ideology behind the modern welfare state through the ideas of mutual obligation and sharing of risks which permeated their activities.

Over the years the attitude of the government to such mutual-benefit organisations has been ambivalent. On the one hand there has been a tendency to welcome them as they seemed to encourage the virtues of thrift, self-reliance and responsibility among the working-classes—virtues dear to the hearts of the Victorians and indeed of the governing classes of most periods of our history. On the other hand there has been a fear that they might exercise an undue influence within society. The chequered history of trade union law is an example of this ambivalence. Again, society has given considerable protection to members of the professions; professional associations can be incorporated; sometimes a Royal Charter confers certain privileges. But there is an uneasy feeling that professional organisations may act as barriers to progress and much-needed reform.

As the social services become more complex, more specialised and subject to a finer division of labour, they become less intelligible to the lay councillor or public representative. A possible consequence is that, collectively, more power may come to reside in the hands of these interests. The question that needs to be asked of professional associations is whether they are prepared to assume greater social responsibilities to match their added knowledge and the power that accompanies it. . . . Professional associations are not the only repositories of knowledge, but they are the repositories of a very special kind of knowledge; and the establishment of proper relations between them and the democratic State is, today, one of the most urgent problems affecting the future of the social services (Titmuss, 1958).

The reference by the President of the Board of Trade of restrictive practices in the professions to the Monopolies Commission in January, 1967, is an indication of public concern about this aspect of professional organisation. There is a growing tendency to increase government control over professional education, particularly in the case of the newer professions and those which are directly concerned with implementation of social policy.

So far only one professional association has been used as an agent by the government to carry out a direct service to the public. The Law Society is responsible for the administration of the Legal Aid and Advice scheme under the Legal Aid and Advice Acts of 1949 and 1960, although the Ministry of Social Security is responsible for determining the financial eligibility for help. Some members of the medical profession have put forward the desirability of a similar arrangement for providing medical services under contract for the National Health Service. It is obvious that difficulties can occur in using organisations whose *primary* reason for existence is the mutual benefit of their members, to provide services for non-members; although they may have subsidiary aims and interests it is equally obvious that the more the interests of the members can be seen to coincide with the interests of the wider community in general and the client group in particular, the more effective will be their use as organs of social policy.

The outstanding example of the use of a mutual-benefit organisation for the implementation of social policy was in the first national health insurance scheme. Under the National Insurance Act, 1911, friendly societies and other mutual-benefit associations could become 'approved' for the purposes of the Act and were responsible for administering sickness benefit. A feature of the scheme which should be noted here was that societies to be approved had to comply with two conditions—they had to be non-profit making and they had to be subject to democratic control by their contributive members.

Blau and Scott (1963) suggest that the crucial issue facing the mutual-benefit association is that of maintaining membership control, that is internal democracy, and they further consider that this involves coping with two main problems, membership apathy and oligarchical control. There have been many studies of these problems, and periodic unrest in this type of organisation is often a sign

38

that, after a period of acquiescence in existing leadership, slipping into apathy when no particularly controversial issues are at stake, the membership wakes up to the situation that power within the organisation has passed into the hands of a few honorary or paid officials who become increasingly out of touch with the interests and wishes of the ordinary members in what may be a period of rapid change. In the case of trade unions this may lead to unofficial strike action, and in the case of professional organisations to breakaway associations. The size and complexity of the organisation has a considerable effect on the reality of internal democratic control. A large association seeking to promote a diversity of objects provides more opportunity for the emergence of policy conflicts often without adequate machinery for the reconciling of the divergent interests of its members.

These various issues were certainly present in the use of 'approved societies' for the administration of the national health scheme. The Royal Commission on National Health Insurance reporting in 1928 commented : 'The vast majority of members, mainly no doubt, by reason of indifference or apathy, do not avail themselves of their opportunities and evince little or no interest in the affairs of their Societies.' The Commission made an interesting point on what they saw as the real social significance of self-government in this kind of mutual-aid organisation.

> The question as it arises in connection with Health Insurance is sometimes spoken of in terms of insured persons looking after their own affairs. This is, we think, to misconceive the point. . . . It is truer to regard the administration of a society as offering an opportunity for public service in the interests of others, and it is safe to say that the great bulk of those who are engaged in the administration of these societies, with older traditions behind them are not in fact consciously looking after their own affairs. They are there because they

desire to find some useful work which they can do for their fellows.

Perhaps democratic control of large mutual-benefit organisations is in truth a myth!

The National Insurance Act, 1946, introduced a unified and more comprehensive system of national insurance administered completely by government organs. William Beveridge, on whose report the main provisions of the new scheme were based, considered that the advantages of direct self-government in social insurance could be bought too dear.

> The smaller the unit, the greater the reality of self-government, but the greater also the disadvantages of any change of residence or employment, such as may be forced on insured persons by economic circumstances. The history of the first thirty years of national health insurance, while it preserves many instances of lively democratic self-help in small societies connected with particular places or trades shows also an unmistakable general tendency towards larger units of administration. . . . Experience and evidence together point the way to making a single Approved Society for the nation (*Social Insurance and Allied Services*, 1962).

The report lists five principal disadvantages for insured persons in addition to the anomaly of unequal benefits for equal contributions and endorses the view of the Royal Commission that the freedom of the insured person to choose the approved society which could best meet his individual needs was more apparent than real. Beveridge's idea of a single Approved Society for the whole population was to a large extent achieved by the Act of 1946 and it is difficult to see the justification for rejecting Beveridge's assessment that in the interests of efficiency and economy the unification of administrative responsibility for social

40

security is essential, which implies a state scheme if any vestige of democratic control is to be maintained.

Different criteria apply when the aims of other mutual benefit associations are considered. Clubs of all kinds flourish in twentieth-century society. Some of these are specific in their aims, being formed to permit the pursuit by their members of some sport or hobby or similar interest; others are concerned with the enhancement of the more general welfare or interests of their members. In most instances social policy contents itself with ensuring that these conform to certain safety and other regulations although there is stricter control of those clubs which come within the licensing or gaming laws. However some kinds of organisations, as for example community associations, women's clubs and sports associations, are actively encouraged by central and local authorities through the provision of subsidies, expert advice and other practical services, under the Physical Training and Recreation Act, 1937, and the Education Act, 1944.

An interesting development of the last twenty years or so has been the spontaneous rise of a number of mutual-aid organisations concerned with the promotion of the welfare of those with a specific mental, physical or social handicap. Usually the primary purpose of such organisations is to give members mutual support and aid, to educate public opinion about their special needs and problems and to act where necessary as pressure groups to influence social policy. The I.P.F. for polio victims, the Cruse Clubs for widows, Alcoholics Anonymous are all examples of this new type of mutual-aid movement. In some of these associations a third problem affecting internal democracy may be identified in addition to those suggested by Blau and Scott—that of the position of individuals (or in some cases of representatives of government agencies) who are interested in the aims of the association but who are not handicapped by the particular disability which unites the other members. A number of the organisations set up to promote the interests of people with specific handicaps or problems permit the enrolment of those who are not themselves handicapped in this way. Usually these are persons with professional interests in the disability—doctors, teachers, social workers, etc., who because of their special expertise may play a dominant role in the organisations and affect the democratic control of the organisation by the ordinary members. Thus some of these organisations hover uncertainly between being mutual benefit and service organisations. Although in practice this uncertainty about 'prime beneficiary' may not affect the eventual welfare of the members yet it can be a source of conflict within the organisation and lead to a breakaway association. Some associations of this type solve the problem by admitting 'non-sufferers' to associate membership only.

This kind of conflict can be seen even more clearly in other fields where the encouragement of clubs and similar associations has become an important part of government policy—both centrally and locally. Are youth organisations and old people's clubs mutual-benefit associations or service organisations? What is the formal relationship between the management committee and the members' committee of the typical youth club? How is the internal organisation affected by the conditions under which grant aid by the local authority is paid?

From this brief discussion of social policy and mutual benefit organisations three things emerge. First, such organisations can have an important part to play in shaping social policy, acting as pressure groups on Parliament and in some instances carrying out a useful function in educating or modifying public opinion. Secondly, from the evidence available it appears that those aspects of social policy which are concerned with providing a service which is open to all citizens on equal terms and guaranteeing at

42

least a minimum standard of benefit are probably more effectively and efficiently pursued through the machinery of public organisation. Thirdly, in other areas of social welfare where the contribution which the individual member himself can make to his own and others' independence, sense of well-being and fellowship is of particular significance, participation in a mutual-benefit association can be of great importance. The size and complexity of organisation in these cases can be crucial.

Social policy can strengthen such associations by sympathetic recognition at both central and local government level, by advice and support and where appropriate by financial assistance, endeavouring to ensure that such help does not endanger the internal democratic government of the organisation.

Business concerns

As already mentioned, social policy may seek to achieve its aims through measures affecting industrial and other business concerns. Blau and Scott predicate that the dominant problem of business concerns is that of operating efficiency, the achievement of maximum gain at the minimum cost in order to further survival and growth in competition with other organisations. Unlike mutual-benefit, commonweal and service organisations, business concerns are expected to place first considerations of operating-efficiency within the limits *externally* imposed on them. Many factory-owners saw disaster for their enterprises on the introduction of factory legislation in the nineteenth century and their modern counterparts frequently prophesy doom as new measures of social action affecting industry are introduced.

The first method by which the government may affect business concerns in the interests of social policy is of course by imposing restrictions on the employment conditions of their workers. The long line of factory Acts has gradually laid down minimum requirements regarding the space, cleanliness, repair and sanitary arrangements in factories and workshops and the guarding of dangerous machinery and other safety precautions. These are under constant review and similar protection has been extended to shop and office workers by the Office, Shops and Railway Premises Act, 1963.

Concern to protect the health and safety particularly of young workers and of women employees has for long been an important aspect of social policy and has been expressed in more positive measures than the regulation of hours of work and the environmental control of working conditions. The Act of 1844 authorised the appointment of Certifying Surgeons responsible for certifying that a child to be employed in a textile factory was of the ordinary strength and appearance of a child of nine years or over. By 1867 they were responsible for medically examining young persons under sixteen starting work in all factories for fitness to work. As codes or regulations for particular hazardous trades and processes were promulgated under which all workers engaged in them were required to undergo periodic medical examinations, so this duty was assigned to the certifying surgeons. From 1948 their modern counterparts, the Appointed Factory Doctors have been required to examine all young persons up to the age of eighteen, when they first take up employment in factories, when they change their employment and at annual intervals. The Appointed Factory Doctor service is largely financed by employers, but it is required by law, and constitutes the major statutory industrial medical service in the country today. Some firms appoint their own works medical officers, and provide a service considerably wider in scope than the statutory minimum.

Other statutory measures which may directly affect the
44

'achievement of maximum gain at minimum cost', are the various social security provisions designed to protect the worker in times of rapid social and economic change. Health and unemployment insurance benefit, graduated pensions and occupational pension schemes all involve employers in financial contributions. Employers must in certain circumstances give due notice of dismissal to a worker under the Contracts of Employment Act, 1963, and give severance pay under the Redundancy Payments Act, 1965. The history of the workmen's compensation acts and industrial injury insurance are interesting examples of the way in which social policy develops. From granting legal protection to certain groups of citizens —in this case workmen employed under a contract of service, compelling employers to provide compensation for the loss of earnings due to accidents arising out of or in the course of their employment—successive governments have gradually moved to a situation in which a compulsory and centrally organised scheme of insurance is financed jointly by employer, employee and the state. The state has not normally interfered in wage-fixing agreements negotiated between employers' representatives and the trade unions except in a few occupations, former 'sweated' trades, which caused so much concern in the early years of this century. There have been some demands for the statutory fixing of a minimum wage in order to counteract the poverty of some families which still exists and for which the imposition of the 'wages stop' is evidence. But except in times of special emergency the government has been reluctant to take and use powers which would interfere in the voluntary nature of wage bargaining even when some members of the community appear to be suffering hardship as a result. It remains to be seen what will be the long-term effect of the Prices and Incomes Act, 1966 in which compulsory powers were taken for a strictly limited time only.

So far we have been considering some of the ways in which the government seeks to implement certain aspects of social policy by imposing limits on the activities of business concerns. In some instances, however, the government uses for its own ends the aims of such concerns. By the use of subsidies on the one hand, and taxation on the other, it can increase or decrease the profitability of certain kinds of production and thus influence profoundly the activities of business concerns. Much of this would appear to be concerned primarily with economic rather than social policy as we have defined it, but attracting new industry to areas of high unemployment under the Distribution of Industry Acts and to new towns by financial and other inducements, subsidising the cost of milk to mothers and children, resulting in greater milk production, encouraging occupational pension schemes through income tax allowances all have as their primary aim the enhancement of social welfare. Moreover the government has become a very large consumer of goods and services produced by private enterprise, and the level of consumer demand has been maintained and its pattern profoundly affected by the transfer payments made under national insurance and other forms of assistance. Again the employment and training services offered by the Ministry of Labour in close association with industry, have had important social as well as economic justification. This is particularly true of the youth employment service and the various provisions for the employable disabled.

For many years successive governments have sought to influence employers to develop services for the welfare of their workers and particularly to have greater regard for good personnel management practices. But it has been suggested that government concern should go deeper than this. The concentration of controlling and decisive powers within industry requires, according to Silburn (1965), 'serious critical examination, particularly from those who

46

believe that in a democracy powers of control should be extended into all areas of a person's life, and that decision-making in the economic and industrial sphere is as fundamental a human right as is decision-making in the political sphere. It may be that our social policy for industry, as it becomes less concerned with questions of survival and more preoccupied with questions of adjustments, should take some active interest in questions of this kind.'

To some people, the nationalisation of certain of our industries in the immediate post-war period presented an opportunity for doing just this type of study without the same kind of pressures as private enterprise is subject to. That this has not been done is probably mostly due to the economic difficulties of the post-war period, and partly to the fact that the government and the country has not yet decided to which category of organisation the nationalised industries belong. Should their primary concern be that of operating efficiency—the achievement of maximum gain at minimum cost—or are they commonweal organisations when consideration of the public good is the predominant concern? The recent controversy over the reorganisation of British Rail and the factors which should be taken into consideration in deciding for instance whether or not a line should be closed, highlights the need to reach some agreement on this basic point before any worthwhile discussion on its future pattern of organisation can be undertaken.

Before we leave consideration of the part to be played by business concerns in the implementation of social policy, we must note again the recent advocacy of an increase in the use of such concerns to provide various forms of 'welfare'. For instance, Seldon (1966) contends that 'if welfare was supplied like consumer services, in response to demand in the market, we should not have the shortages in schools, teachers, hospitals, doctors and nurses that tax-financed state welfare has left as its legacy'.

47

There are a number of organisations offering personal services run on a profit-making basis, for example, schools, nursing-home, private medical care and most of our legal advice, and commercial insurance covers every conceivable type of risk. It is difficult to judge whether an increase in the business section of 'welfare' would necessarily lead to more real choice on the part of the consumer, to a greater supply of it or a more efficient use of scarce resources as has been argued. Certainly past experience and the situation in other countries is not particularly reassuring. Indeed is it possible to speak of 'welfare' as a consumer commodity? Moreover, the arguments for this reversal of the developments which have taken place over the last half-century would seem to be based on the view that these welfare needs are the private concern of the individual citizen whereas it can be equally argued that society also has an important stake in the well-being of its citizens. Blau and Scott argue that the traditional professional practitioner who makes a living by collecting fees from his clients comes into conflict with the requirement to set self-interest aside in rendering service to them. They suggest that as the salaried professional in a service organisation supported by community or philanthropic funds is free of this pressure these conditions would seem to be more conducive to promoting disinterested service.

Another area of government policy where there is a considerable lack of unanimity is that of housing. Using our categories of organisation once more—should housing departments consider themselves as business concerns, commonweal or service organisations? A family's need for shelter entails the provision not only of a house or flat, but also of land on which to put it and many communal facilities, shops, schools, libraries, cinemas, dance-halls, bowling alleys, etc., as well as a place to work and a countryside to enjoy. Thus inevitably housing has been linked with the need to undertake the task of planning the use of our basic natural resource—that of land—for the benefit of the community as a whole.

Commonweal organisations

In Blau and Scott's classification, the distinctive characteristics of commonweal organisations is that the public-at-large is the primary beneficiary, often, although not necessarily, to the exclusion of the very people who are the object of the organisation's activities. The press is full of reports of individuals and families who may have to move their homes or give up land in order to provide necessary facilities such as roads, houses or new shopping areas in the interests of the community. The police service is for the protection of the public, the maintenance of law and order, but their activities may be detrimental to the immediate welfare of the individual criminal!

Most of the 'commonweal' organisations either perform protective services for the community or serve as its administrative arm. Thus most but not all central government departments and local authorities fall into this category. We have already noted that certain aims of social policy are achieved through business concerns and mutual-benefit associations. But of course there has to be some government agency which is responsible for framing the appropriate legislation, drawing up any necessary regulations and ensuring that the policy so expressed is in fact implemented. Thus the Ministry of Labour, through its Safety, Health and Welfare Department, is responsible for ensuring that employers carry out the many regulations concerning the maintenance of the health and safety of factory workers; the Ministry of Social Security is responsible for ensuring that employing bodies comply with the terms of the national insurance and related acts; the Board of Trade and the Registrar of Friendly Societies have important functions in regard to certain mutual-benefit

49

associations; the Commissioners of Inland Revenue play an increasing part in implementing the social aspects of fiscal policy.

In recent years there has been increasing interest on the part of the government in the possibilities of planning changes in the physical environment for the benefit of the public as a whole. This is partly due to the problems posed by an expanding population within a country of limited size and few natural resources. Historically public concern has developed from an attempt to replace slum dwellings by more convenient and better standard houses for the working classes, through an interest in planning new council estates, the creation of neighbourhoods or communities, to the designing of new towns and a growing concern for the creation and preservation of areas of natural amenity and particular beauty. It was not until the period between the two world wars that local authorities acquired any significant powers for the provision of houses and thus had the opportunity of creating new communities which would combine a good standard of housing with easy access to shops, schools and other amenities. That little use was made of the principles and ideas of pioneers such as Ebenezer Howard is evidenced by the existence of so many housing estates, built both during this period and since 1945, which lack amenities, and which have added to the problems of ribbon development, emphasising the already existing suburban sprawl of most towns and cities. Much of this urban sprawl and the growth of industrial black spots has been the result of unregulated private building—unregulated, that is, in regard to the siting and planning of new houses as long as they complied with public health requirements.

A new impetus was given to the whole concept of planning by the publication of three reports in the early 1940's. A Royal Commission on the Distribution of the Industrial Population under the chairmanship of Sir Montague Barlow had been set up in 1937 and issued its report in 1940. The main recommendation of this report was that efforts should be made to control the drift to the south-east and the continued expansion of large towns by a planned dispersal of population to new towns. Such measures obviously needed a central planning authority and in 1943 the Ministry of Town and Country Planning was brought into being to give effect to the recommendations in this and two other related reports, that of the Committee on Land Utilisation in Rural Areas (the Scott Committee), and that on Compensation and Betterment (the Uthwatt Committee). The statutory basis of the new initiative in planning was the three Acts, the Town and Country Planning Act, 1947, the New Towns Act, 1946 and the Town Development Act, 1952. The opportunity for creating new city centres was made possible by the widespread destruction caused by bombing during the war and many cities and towns have been able to plan and develop such centres as a whole. This concept of positive planning was given legislative recognition in the Town and Country Planning Act, 1944 which first enabled local authorities to undertake comprehensive redevelopment not only of areas damaged by enemy action but also of those affected by 'blight' in the sense of being obsolete or obsolescent. Some such plans have been completed only after long and protracted negotiation over compensation for land acquired under compulsory purchase orders. In other situations the power of the local authorities over the planning of their areas is primarily negative in character. The Act of 1947 required county and county borough councils to prepare 'Development Plans' setting out their suggestions for the long-term use of land within their boundaries and once the Plan was approved by the central government it became a statutory instrument with the force of law and the basis of planning control. Every change in the use of land and all new buildings and additions became subject

51

to control by the local authorities who could only give permission if it was in accordance with the plan. Local authorities are required to make a new survey at least every five years and adapt their plans if this seems advisable in the light of our rapidly changing society.

Centrally, the organ of control has been the Minister of Housing and Local Government since 1951 when the Ministry of Town and Country Planning was dissolved. To safeguard the rights of the individual citizen and of interested groups, there is a right of appeal to the Minister. Another development which should perhaps be mentioned is the setting up of the National Parks Commission and the Nature Conservancy Board under the National Parks and Access to the Countryside Act, 1949. Recently the whole concept of planning has broadened with the setting up of a planning unit under the new Ministry of Economic Affairs. This co-operates closely with the other ministries in regional planning boards, and with the economic planning councils for each major region which include members of the general public, representatives of industry, of the trades unions, of the universities and of local government. A number of studies have resulted from these developments but it is still too early to determine the effectiveness of the new machinery. There are signs that some local authorities are uncertain of their own role in relation to the new bodies and are concerned at the threat to existing powers of local authorities implied in the new emphasis on regionalism.

The whole concept of planning in this comprehensive way is a subject of bitter controversy, and highlights the difficulties inherent in the operation of all organisations concerned with promoting the commonweal—the problems of deciding between conflicting interests and between short- and long-term benefits. The shortage of land in relation to population has made these problems particularly acute in Britain and controversy over its use is perhaps one of the most politically explosive questions at present. The development of the idea of regionalism has brought to the fore the problem of the democratic control of new regional machinery. Indeed, Blau and Scott consider that this is the crucial problem for all commonweal organisation. While external democratic control is essential, the internal structure of these organisations, they suggest, is expected to be bureaucratic, governed by the criterion of efficiency. In this country there has been a long tradition of local government, and as we have seen, much social policy is implemented at local level through elected district and borough councils and through county and county borough councils. Even though the powers of such authorities are limited by statute they have considerable freedom to interpret much legislation and to determine how it will be implemented locally. In theory at least the councils and their committees are responsible for the quality of local services and their chief officers are their servants. The relationship between administrators and committees is a study in itself but as the business of government becomes more complex the expert chief officer is likely in practice to develop considerable power both within his department and in influencing his committee, comprised usually of non-experts. In the same way, it is difficult to estimate the power of the Civil Service to influence policy as well as determining the methods of its implementation. Even though the Government may take decisions on major policy issues, the effectiveness of these decisions will depend upon many other decisions taken at all levels of the administrative hierarchy. In the long run it is the vigilance of the citizen body and their elected representatives that must ensure effective democratic control over those organisations, departments of state, local authorities and *ad hoc* boards which are responsible for promoting the commonweal. Public audit, the select committee on the estimates, committees and commissions of inquiry are all

53

means which, if used properly, should strengthen the control of the electorate over the administration and help to make available the information on which constructive criticism can be based.

Service organisations

The development of the 'service' organisation whose aim is the welfare of its clients has been a characteristic result of social policy in the last half-century. The extension of statutory provision designed to provide for the needs of groups of client citizens has grown out of the work of numerous voluntary organisations with a concern for those in the community in special need or with particularly difficult problems. Such organisations have tended to be provided and run by the 'better-off' members of the community for those considered to be under-privileged or deprived in some way, and have taken many forms and some mention has already been made of these in Chapter 2. Although the motives of the givers may be suspect in some instances and in all cases are likely to be mixed, yet the explicit reason for the establishment of such voluntary societies has been the welfare of the recipient. The factors leading to the establishment of many of the statutory social services have been more complex. The establishment of the school meals service, the school health service, the development of the maternity and child welfare services were all seen in part at least as the answer to the findings of the Inter-Departmental Committee on the Physical Deterioration of the Young which reported in 1904 and investigated why so many of the recruits for the Boer War were rejected as unfit. Secondary education of all kinds, and particularly technical education, is seen today as being of crucial importance to the future economic progress of the community, and not only the right of the individual. A case can be made out for including many of the personal social

54

services in the category of commonweal organisations, for it would seem that their primary concern is the saving to the community as a whole of the cost of broken homes, of increased delinquency or mental ill-health by meeting the needs of groups who are considered to be 'at risk'. Indeed, historically, statutory provision has largely resulted from the recognition of the social and economic effects of individual ill-health, bad housing, poor education, poverty, unemployment, marital disharmony and child neglect. It is perhaps significant that those services which do not have, or are not easily seen to have, this kind of immediate benefit for the common good usually have less claim on public funds. Some of the biggest gaps in social provision seem to be in services for the unemployable handicapped, for old people, and for those with marital problems. Periodically public opinion is stirred and action is demanded as the result of some scandal or disaster, action which would otherwise be opposed as too costly, unnecessary or constituting unwarrantable interference. The disaster of Aberfan in 1966 stirred many people to words and action who would not have been prepared to pay higher taxes, higher rates or an increased price for coal to *prevent* such disasters, or to make all mining areas more healthy and attractive places in which to live.

Nevertheless, although the welfare of the society as a whole must always be an important consideration in the development and working of the social services—if only because of the problem of priorities in a world of scarce resources—it is probably true to say that government, administrators and the public-at-large are increasingly agreed that the social services should be seen as having as their prime beneficiary the client group, that the welfare of the recipient should be the major factor in the organisation of the service. This concept indeed finds its way into legislation and for example the Social Security Act, 1966 as also the National Assistance Act, 1948, states that the Supplementary Benefits Commission shall exercise their functions 'in such a manner as shall best promote the welfare of persons affected'. That this must not be taken for granted can be seen if the procedures and standard of provision of the average child-care service is contrasted with the treatment of homeless families.

The concept of comprehensive services available to all citizens on like terms, which has been one of the dynamic ideas creating the Welfare State, has had a profound effect on the organisation of the social services. Not only has it meant a great increase in the size and complexity of the organisation necessary but it has led to an insistent demand that the standard of service provided by such organisations should be at the optimum level consistent with the resources available rather than a tolerable minimum. When education and medical services provided by the state were primarily intended for the less fortunate or underprivileged members of society who had no claim save that of charity, there was little public demand for a high standard of service. Today, when every citizen has a right to any necessary medical care, and when every child can claim education according to age, ability and aptitude, there is an insistent demand for the improvement of these services. The creation of such organisations as The Patients Association, The Association for the Improvement of the Maternity Services, The Association for the Advancement of State Education are examples of the way in which the 'client' group, now including more articulate and politically conscious citizens, is concerned to improve the standard of service organisations. The development of the principle of universalisation has meant that there has been ever-increasing recognition that such services are a national rather than a local financial responsibility, with a consequent growth of central control. Those services which are available to all and used by all citizens at some time in their lives tend to be those which are administered by a central government department such as the Ministry of Social Security and the Ministry of Labour or those where the central body is the dominant partner as are the Department of Education and Science and the Ministry of Health. We have already noted in a previous chapter that one of the problems of services which are administered by local authorities is that they tend to be uneven in their standards, and differences in availability of social resources do not necessarily appear to be associated with genuine differences in local needs. Thus a demand for greater equality of treatment and availability of resources leads to increased demand for central government control.

In opposition to this is the view strongly held by some people that in the interests of democracy, local government must be strengthened. As more public services are becoming the responsibility of regional boards or councils, there has been a tendency to see in the provision of the personal services a means to strengthen local government by increasing the powers even of the minor authorities. The danger of administering the personal health services, the welfare and children's services by large 'impersonal' authorities has thus tended to be stressed. This view was seen for instance in the report of the Royal Commission on Local Government in Greater London and in the provision of the Local Government Act, 1958 which required the delegation by the county councils of certain health and welfare functions to the borough and district councils of more than sixty thousand inhabitants.

There is little factual evidence that the personal social services necessarily require to be administered in small local areas or by elected authorities, although much expert opinion expressed for instance in some of the evidence presented to the Seebohm Committee, holds that it is helpful to clients, workers and the public-at-large if there are local offices providing ease of access. This does not necessarily mean that the main unit of administration has to

57

be local, as the organisation of the Ministry of Social Security and the Ministry of Labour demonstrate. One of the main reasons for the creation of the Unemployment Assistance Board under the Act of 1934 was the desire to remove the giving of assistance based upon assessment of individual need from the maelstrom of party politics, both national and local, and ensure the confidential and discretionary nature of the assessment based on ascertained need. Some critics of the present local government responsibility for the personal social services would draw a parallel here and argue that these too would be better administered by a national *ad hoc* body. The provision of professional services and the maintenance of privacy and confidentiality may not be easily reconcilable with traditional local authority committee procedure or the local councillor's role as an elected representative.

Another factor of some importance must however be considered. In recent years the concept of 'community care' for the mentally and physically handicapped, for the old and others requiring special help has dominated much of the thinking and planning of those responsible for meeting the needs of these groups. Increasingly community care is seen not only as the provision of homes, hostels, work and social centres, the assistance of skilled domiciliary help of many kinds, but also the involvement of family, friends and neighbours in a co-operative attempt to retain as many disabled or infirm people as possible in the local community. To be successful this policy requires much educational and supportive work within the local area and, it is suggested, the most effective means of ensuring this is to make the community feel responsible for the services through its elected local councillors.

Blau and Scott suggest that the crucial problem in 'service' organisations is their employment of professional workers and the relationship of the professional practitioner and the administrator. Much of the conflict that

58

occurs in the organisation and development of the personal social services seems to centre round this problem; medical practitioners in general practice have been particularly fearful of administrative interference. The Executive Councils and payment on a *per capita* basis are compromise devices designed to allay the fears of general practitioners that employment by local health authorities and a salaried service would rob them of their professional independence. Thus arise some of the anomalies of the present organisation of the National Health Service. Blau and Scott appear to restrict their discussion of professional people in 'service' organisations to those who characteristically provide direct expert services to 'clients', who have a deep commitment to their professional colleagues and who organise themselves into voluntary associations for the purpose of professional control. However, not all 'service' organisations necessarily make extensive use of professional people if 'professional' is interpreted in this sense.

The benefit to the individual citizen from the operation of some 'service' organisations comes from the use of a number of resources, perhaps a combination of practical aid, financial assistance and technical skill brought together and 'mediated' by a field-worker or some other official in personal contact with the individual. Thus the needs of a disabled person may be met by the provision of some mechanical aid to greater mobility, the provision of suitable pastime occupation either at home or at a local centre, help in obtaining and paying for suitable holiday accommodation for himself and his family, and information and advice in his fight to become more independent and to live as full a life in the community as possible. The help, technical knowledge and skill of a number of different persons both within and outside the organisation may be necessary for these needs of the individual to be met. The problem of conflicting loyalties of professional *versus* administrative decisions may never arise, as it is the or-

59

ganisation as a whole which is providing the 'service' rather than an individual professional practitioner. Although one worker may have to accept responsibility for co-ordinating the contribution of others and for mobilising the necessary resources, the traditional professional-client relationship may be less appropriate than a service-citizen relationship.

A more general problem, but one of increasing importance, is that of the mounting cost of service organisations —one shared by 'service' industries. Just because their effectiveness depends primarily upon the personal skill and knowledge of the workers in the organisation, the maintenance or raising of standards of service and the extension of facilities depend upon the ability to recruit sufficient people of the appropriate calibre and to obtain adequate financial resources to pay for them. In a society where the emphasis tends to be on ever-increasing technological advance, greater productivity per man-hour, rising standards and expectation of affluence, the service industries find themselves in a dilemma. There is less scope for the employment of labour-saving techniques than in other industries and at a time when wages and salaries are rising increasing affluence on the part of consumers tends to make greater demands on such 'service' industries. In business concerns rising demand can lead to higher prices but in the 'service' organisations providing personal help of many kinds to client citizens, rising costs cause difficulties which lead to a questioning of the whole basis of the Welfare State.

5

Policy, process and personnel

In the field of social policy as in other areas of decision-making—indeed perhaps more than in other areas—means and ends cannot in practice be easily distinguished; policy and process are often inextricably intertwined. The growth in interest in social administration as a subject of academic study as well as 'a process directed to the solution of social problems, the promotion of social welfare or the implementation of social policy' (Slack, 1966) is perhaps witness to the growing realisation that the *way* in which a service is administered is often as important to the recipient as *what* is administered. In a pamphlet published in 1948, Arthur Radford wrote, 'Giving people bread is not necessarily a social service for a social service is performed with no impairment of the beneficiary's social dignity or status'. The institution of the 'means test' in the financial crisis of 1931 was meant, from a social point of view, to underline the importance of family responsibility but in fact the way in which it was carried out led to the physical splitting up of families, threatening rather than strengthening family cohesion. Again, the preamble to the National Health Service Act stated that its aim was to provide a comprehensive health service designed to secure improvement in the physical and mental health of the people. This policy is nullified if people are deterred from seeking advice from their doctors at an early stage either because the organisation of the service is such that there is no ease of access to adequate diagnostic facilities or if the patient feels that he may be labelled a malingerer or hypochondriac if he seeks advice before his symptoms of illness have become obvious. Thus the effectiveness of any service depends not only upon its structure but also upon procedures and personnel.

The way in which decisions made in the course of the administrative process subsequently modify or lead to important developments in the original policies themselves is now generally recognised and is demonstrated in the case studies described and analysed in Donnison, *Social Policy and Administration*.

The kind of processes involved in the implementation of social policy will vary according to the actual policy under consideration. Some writers have concluded that there are few common factors because the process of administration is so complex and only has validity in the light of the ends to be achieved. There is some truth in this view but it is perhaps possible to distinguish three main categories of social action and several sub-sections within which the processes of administration have some common features, based on the *kind* of decisions that have to be made during the administrative process and *where* they are made in the organisational hierarchy.

Control by regulation and subsidy

First there are those aspects of social policy which are concerned with the discouragement or encouragement of certain kinds of behaviour on the part of employers, workers, consumers or other groups or the public-at-large, through prohibition, through direct or indirect subsidies

62

or through the taxation system. These require the formulation of regulations laying down the kind of action that is prohibited or to be encouraged, or the circumstances in which help may be given. Such requirements may be embodied in Acts of Parliament or in statutory regulations made under the Acts, and are usually enforceable in the last resort through the courts. Much factory and public health legislation is of this kind.

This category of social action necessitates first of all the careful drafting of regulations setting out clearly the precise situations in which for instance an employing body be required to provide safety guards for dangerous machinery or a landlord adequate toilet facilities or access to a pure water supply for his tenants, or in which a superannuation scheme can be accepted for an allowance for income tax purposes. This is the job of senior civil servants often on the basis of information obtained from special inquiries, reports from ministry inspectors and advice from other experts. If regulations are accepted by Parliament and become statutory instruments, then responsibility for seeing that they are carried out usually rests with an inspectorate appointed by the appropriate ministry or local authority. From 1833 when the first provision was made for independent factory inspectors to be appointed, doctors, lawyers, educationalists, scientists and technical experts of all kinds have brought a new element into both central and local government administration. It was largely they who were responsible for seeing that policy laid down by Parliament was implemented and adequate standards attained by local factory-owners, voluntary school societies, local public health authorities, prison governors and lunatic asylum superintendents. Today their work is even more important as the sphere of state interest has broadened.

The giving of information and advice to those affected by social legislation, and the feeding back to those in a

63

position to influence future policy is an important part of the job of the inspectors and other central and local government officers. Primarily however the process involved is one of investigation, of ascertaining whether the relevant rules have been observed and taking appropriate action in cases of any breach. Decisions are made in accordance with more or less clearly defined rules and regulations; such an administrative process calls for officials with detailed knowledge of the relevant regulations, a meticulous attention to the facts of the situation and the ability to set in motion the machinery for the enforcement of regulations where necessary. The Factory Acts of 1802 and 1819 were virtually dead letters because their enforcement was in the hands of the local Justices of the Peace, who were often interested parties. Regulations which seem irksome to those they affect will only be accepted if they are seen to be enforced fairly and without discrimination. Any inspectorate to be successful must be as impartial as is humanly possible—and be seen to be so; at the same time, much of their work is carried out through the giving of informal advice and help, and is thus a job requiring integrity and good judgement as well as skill and knowledge.

Inspectors are, of course, also used by central government departments to maintain some uniformity of provision and standard by the local authorities and other public agencies. As Herman Finer has suggested, 'They are the "in-between" men and women, in the service of the central department to watch, record and report the local state of affairs to convey the intentions and will of the centre, and the predicaments of the peripheries' (from a Foreword to J. S. Harris, *The British Government Inspectors*, 1955). In the same way local education authorities themselves appoint both general and specialist inspectors and advisers to give help, advice and supervision to schools, clubs and other institutions.

Planning procedures

Direct and indirect social action through statutory regulations, through subsidies and through taxation are assum-
ing new proportions and becoming more complex as the
result of the increased attempts at large-scale social and
economic planning. Such planning is necessitated by the
growing complexity of industrialised and urbanised society
and by the pressure of an increasing population on scarce
resources particularly of land. The unsatisfactory nature
of much planning in the past has forced a reappraisal of
methods and content of planning and the recognition of
three essential ingredients: the collection of adequate relevant data, the studying and planning of resources in the
light of this data and of the goals to be achieved, and the
implementation of these plans through regulation and
other forms of action.

The beginning of a new era in public administration
was perhaps marked by the preparation and publication
of the first three regional plans, on Central Scotland produced by the Scottish Development Department, on North
East England by an inter-departmental team (both in 1963)
and that on the south-east by the Ministry of Housing and
Local Government in 1964. This was followed by the setting up of a new Department of Economic Affairs, the
publication in 1965 of the National Plan, and the inauguration of new regional machinery consisting of Economic
Planning Councils and Economic Planning Boards. The
studies which have resulted are attempts at providing the
data for successful comprehensive planning, combining
economic, social and physical factors. The preparation of
the studies themselves offers interesting examples of co-
operation between many different bodies and individuals.
As the Foreword to the East Midlands Study states:

The Study has largely been prepared by the Regional

Economic Planning Board with the advice and help of the Regional Economic Planning Council as the work progressed. It could only however have been compiled with the assistance which has been freely given by everyone who has been approached—local authorities, large and small, nationalised industries and public utility undertakings, very many private firms and the trade associations.

Both centrally and regionally the new interest in planning has meant the increasing development and use by the government of its own teams of experts, and less reliance on private firms of consultants for reports and plans for particular projects.

Considerable progress is already being made in putting into effect some of the proposals arising out of earlier studies, and their resulting plans. Reference was made earlier to the use of the public corporation to plan and build new areas of population under the New Towns Acts. The setting up of the Commission for the New Towns under the Act of 1959 to take over certain functions from the Development Corporations as each new town nears completion is an interesting attempt to help these areas to achieve 'normality'. Unlike the corporations, the Commission, with a small headquarters staff to maintain general control over policy, finance and capital investment, delegates the execution of this policy and the detailed management of its local housing, commercial and industrial assets to a manager in the particular town. This transitional stage when new towns are no longer new but are not yet fully developed continues to cause problems of relationship between the Commission and the local authorities although, unlike a development corporation whose powers to some extent duplicate those of the local authorities, the commission's functions do not overlap those of the latter.

Various methods are used to achieve some of the special

programmes of economic and social development in 'problem' areas. Broadly the policy to stimulate new industrial development in those areas of relatively high unemployment, population loss and inadequate social amenities has resulted in powers being given to the Board of Trade under the Industrial Development Act, 1966 to define development areas, to effect a redistribution of industry by a system of industrial development certificates and to induce new industries through investment grants, building grants and the provision of factory premises for rent or sale on favourable terms. Parallel to this the Ministry of Labour under the Employment and Training Act has schemes for providing financial and direct assistance for the training of new labour needed by firms in the development areas.

Much planning activity still centres round the work of the Ministry of Housing and Local Government, in relation to Town and Country Planning and the responsibilities of the local authorities in this field. There are two main aspects of this, the preparation, submission and approval of development plans, their review and amendment, and development control for which machinery is set in motion by a person applying for permission to develop land. The Planning Divisions within the Ministry bear the main responsibility for the Department's planning policy and for the administration of the planning system. These divisions are staffed entirely by civil servants with no technical expertise. The Planning Services Division, however, provides a professional service on planning matters to advise the administrators. Its role is threefold: it gives expert advice and evaluation to the Planning Divisions and any other part of the Department as required; it carries out research into planning problems; and it acts as the Department's main link with the local planning authorities, county and county borough councils. Almost all the counties have a separate planning officer with professional qualifications who is of chief officer status, but the situation in county boroughs is different since there are few separate planning officers. Where there is no separate planning officer, there is a danger that planning considerations may be subordinated to other interests. In making development plans the advice or even the informal pressure of the regional planning officers may be a most important factor in the decision by the local authorities as to what the development plan shall contain. After formal submission the plan is usually the subject of a local inquiry by a member of the Ministry's inspectorate. Such inspectors normally have relevant professional qualifications. They have considerable independence, and have a quasi-judicial function. It is their job to preside at inquiries and hearings relating to compulsory purchase orders, slum-clearance orders, development plans, planning appeals, advertisement appeals, etc., and make reports to the Ministry, but it is the administrators in the department who make the final decision.

The relationship between the Ministry and local planning authorities is complicated by the fact that the former has a general interest—as the department responsible for planning—in the development plans and decisions of the latter, but because the rights of individuals are involved especially in planning appeals, the Department is also required to decide between local planning authorities and those individuals. New procedures are being worked out to give individuals protection from undue hardships but at the same time enable decisions to be reached more speedily than in the past.

Another area where there have been attempts recently to improve the machinery for planning for future needs is in the health and welfare services. Thus the publication of *A Hospital Plan for England and Wales*, 1962 and of *Health and Welfare: the Development of Community Care*, 1963 by the Ministry of Health were attempts to plan more realistically for the 1970's in the health and welfare

68

services. The latter plan shows wide variations in the estimated requirements for staff, for all kinds of residential accommodation and for day-care facilities apparently not related to local differences in need due to local conditions. These variations are nearly as great in the older established services such as maternal and child welfare as in the newer ones for the physically handicapped. This suggests that facilities for the collection and analysis of data from which realistic plans for future development can be made are surprisingly inadequate. In the case of the hospitals, the creation of the Regional Hospital Boards under the National Health Service Act, 1946, charged with responsibility for keeping the needs of their areas under constant review and for planning comprehensive hospital facilities and consultant services, perhaps enabled the Hospital Plan to be more effective although economic difficulties have prevented its full implementation.

The size and nature of the problems concerned with comprehensive planning in a rapidly changing situation demand flexibility of approach, constant reappraisal of needs and of other relevant factors, the increasing use of highly qualified and skilled specialist planners and the creation of multi-disciplined teams. It also requires the involvement of the public in planning at all stages and a process of social education which enables individuals to understand, appreciate and indeed to contribute to the aims and methods of planning in a complex society.

The social services: meeting individual need

The third category of social action is concerned with providing direct benefits to individuals or groups in the community and comprises the social services. Today these cover many different forms of help.

First we can distinguish social action providing benefits to which citizens are entitled by virtue of an actual or

69

implied contract. Thus national insurance benefits are payable to those who have contributed to the scheme under certain specified and predetermined conditions laid down by Parliament and amplified by regulations. Theoretically the establishment of eligibility for benefit and its payment can be carried out by an administrative process involving little personal contact between recipient and official. In actuality the complexity of many of the regulations and of the situations they are designed to meet is such that numerous queries about contributions and benefits have to be sorted out, involving personal interviews at local offices of the Ministry. However, decisions taken by most of the officials are decisions concerning facts—whether or not applications are in order and whether eligibility has been established according to the rules; these rules are so numerous and intricate that there is considerable specialisation of officers within the service. Provision is made in the National Insurance Acts for the reference of disputed decisions about eligibility or amount of benefit or where regulations do not quite fit individuals' circumstances, to local tribunals or to a Commissioner.

It must be noted that the Ministry relies to a considerable extent on the co-operation of other bodies and individuals to establish the eligibility of applicants. It is the Department's responsibility to keep records of the contributions made by insured persons—now virtually the whole population of working age—but eligibility for unemployment benefit is indicated by signing on at the Employment Exchange, and a medical certificate is required for establishing a right to sickness benefit, maternity benefit, etc. The use of other agencies to establish eligibility except in certain long-term or disputed cases means that the administrative processes involved in the internal organisation of national insurance are comparatively straightforward.

The taking over by the Ministry of Social Security from

the National Assistance Board of responsibility for providing assistance to those whose resources are inadequate to meet their needs, however, introduced a new element into the department. The payment of supplementary benefits entails a personal and individual inquiry into the situation of the applicant to ensure that all relevant sources of income and all appropriate needs are disclosed. The judgement of the officer concerned is required to estimate the kind and degree of assistance that should be given, particularly if this involves additional payments over and above the usual scale of supplementary benefit, or referral to other departments or voluntary agencies. Workers undertaking this kind of personal investigation must develop special skills and knowledge and the success of the service depends in a very real way on them.

This emphasis on the importance of the person who is at the point of contact between the service and the citizen is found in many other organisations. As each new service has developed it has tended to create its own specialised workers to mediate the service, to establish eligibility and to ensure the welfare of the recipient. The provision of aids to the handicapped, of home helps, of meals on wheels and many other forms of domiciliary help and of residential provision are examples where the process of administration relies on the judgement and knowledge of these field-workers and there is an increasing demand for organised courses of training for them.

There has also been a recognition of the help that can be given to individuals and groups by a skilled worker through the creation and utilisation of a professional relationship. Social workers are primarily concerned with helping people to live fuller and more worthwhile lives. In the past this mostly took the form of providing for the needs of the underprivileged. As these needs have begun to be met either by the rise in the general standard of living or by more general community provision, social workers

71

have moved on to the realisation that many people still have problems which are not solved by better material standards or the availability of social resources. Thus new methods of help have 'evolved from the gradually accumulated experience of social work teachers and practitioners in this (probation) and other fields as they have learnt to apply and test a growing body of psychological and sociological theory' (*Report of The Departmental Committee on the Probation Service*, 1962). Although social casework as a method of social work has gone further in developing a more coherent body of theory and practice in recent years, group work and community organisation are also beginning to be accepted as methods of professional social work. These methods, pioneered by some of the older-established professional social work groups—family caseworkers, psychiatric social workers, almoners and probation officers —are gradually permeating a variety of services and affecting the practice of many field-workers·

The marriage of two traditions, the one which may be called 'client-centred' and the other 'service-centred' has led to a difficult phase of mutual adjustment. There is still insufficient recognition that administrative procedures inherited from the past, which were valid for the conduct of impersonal services or those giving material help to clearly defined categories of need, are not always suitable when dealing with the personal problems of individuals. In some services the primary function of the field worker is to facilitate the provision of various forms of material aid; in others their function is to give direct help with personal problems of relationship and adjustment of an intangible kind—and thus the organisation exists to facilitate their work. This has presumably always been true of probation departments where administrative procedures are concerned to provide the optimum conditions within which probation officers, who are directly responsible to the courts, can carry out their job 'to advise, assist and

72

befriend' those probationers placed in their care. In this kind of department the structure and procedures of the organisation will be different from that, for instance, of a local authority welfare department providing residential and day care for the physically handicapped, and for elderly and infirm people, and many different kinds of practical aids to mobility, occupation and social centres and other forms of domiciliary assistance.

Changes in the functions of organisations can cause considerable stresses within their administrative framework while new formal relationships and new procedures are worked out. Thus since their establishment in 1948 there have been very great changes in the responsibilities and work of the local authority children's departments. These have placed more responsibility on the field-workers and emphasised the importance of their knowledge and skill, for it is mainly by personal work with families at risk that home conditions can be improved or at least prevented from deteriorating. This development may call for a re-alignment of administrative and professional responsibilities within such departments. The field-worker is moving from a primary concern to establish 'eligibility' for taking into care and to arrange fostering or reception into a Home: now the primary concern is to work with families in their own homes. Thus as in 'clinical' services, the help offered is pre-eminently the specialised knowledge and skill of a professional worker, and the administration of the department must play a supporting role, as we have already suggested it should in a probation department. The provision of foster care, of boarding education, of hostel accommodation are then seen as part of the total social resources at the disposal of the worker to be used selectively according to the needs of the family concerned; this may demand a much greater degree of individual responsibility being placed on—and being accepted by—the field-worker.

73

Professional people in formal organisations

This leads on to a consideration of the place of professional people in formal organisations. Over the last hundred years the Civil Service has increasingly recruited a variety of people with professional qualifications to give expert advice in the forming of policy, in framing legislation or regulations and in carrying out certain specialist services in the inspectorate. Mackenzie and Grove (1957) point out that

> The organisation which represents many of the specialist classes is called the Institution of Professional Civil Servants, and by this is implied that the members of the specialist classes are in the first place members of a recognised profession or craft, and then in the second place members of the Civil Service. Perhaps members of the 'general' classes are more truly 'professional civil servants', since few of them owe allegiance to any profession except the Civil Service and their skills do not give personal standing outside the service.

Acute problems have arisen with the development of the personal social services and the increasing use of professional people, doctors, nurses, teachers, and social workers to provide skilled help through public agencies.

Blau and Scott (1963) consider that professional expertness and bureaucratic discipline may be viewed as alternative methods of coping with areas of uncertainty. Bureaucratic discipline does so by reducing the scope of uncertainty; expertness, by providing the knowledge and social support through the professional peer group that enable individuals to cope with uncertainty and thus assume more responsibility. The meticulous carrying out of regulations and the endorsement of action by an administrative superior may give security to a worker operating in an area where decisions and consequent

74

action may have grave and far-reaching repercussions. Some employees of public departments—both central and local—may welcome the sense of support and security which comes from working within a well-ordered hierarchy of authority and procedure; others find such a setting frustrating and inhibiting. Thus some child-care officers are happier with the knowledge that there are regulations with which they have to comply, for instance, in the visiting of foster-children and the forms that may have to be completed before certain kinds of action can be taken. Others increasingly see their job as one in which professional knowledge and skills have to be used and in which they must be prepared to take responsibility for decisions lying within their field of professional competence. These may find the administrative structure and methods of procedure in some departments to be destructive of their feeling of responsibility and threatening to the standard of professional help they can offer to their clients. Blau and Scott (1963) found that 'Apparently an orientation to the profession as a reference group makes a worker somewhat independent of organisational pressures and thus more inclined to deviate from administrative procedures in the interests of professional service to clients'.

The difficulties that may arise for the members of a profession when the state becomes the largest employer of their services is something about which medical practitioners have been concerned since the inauguration of a national health insurance scheme under the National Insurance Act, 1911. Some of these discussions have been complicated by a failure to recognise other trends at work. For instance the increase in knowledge and the consequent acceleration of specialisation complicates the problem of responsibility and accountability. Thus the complaint that the National Health Service is undermining the position of the family doctor does not seem to be justified. The most serious threat comes from the spectacular developments in medical science which mean that it is no longer possible for a doctor on his own to treat adequately more than a fraction of his patients. He must make increasing use of specialist consultants and ancillary workers. The traditional concept of the responsibility of the individual doctor for his patient is becoming irrelevant and as yet too little attention appears to have been given to the alternative concept of group or team responsibility and the organisational and decision-making problems involved. Specialisation of function entails co-ordination and as Simon (1957) points out 'When co-ordination goes further than mere communication, when it deliberately influences the behaviour of group members in desired directions, it ordinarily involves some measure of authority'. The authority and accountability problems inherent in the development of specialisation in medical science are to some extent masked by the present tripartite administrative division of the National Health Service. Reorganisation would demand a considerable amount of rethinking about decision-making and the nature of professional responsibility. Though the division of responsibility between medical practitioner and lay administrator or local committee has been the bugbear of many members of the medical profession, the real problems may lie between general practitioner and specialist or between specialist and specialist. The bogy that the 'socialisation' of the medical profession would result in lay dominance and the loss of professional freedom is shown by Stevens (1966) to be completely unreal; as at present organised, professional representation is dominant throughout the administration of the health service.

The experience of other professional groups has been different. Local authorities have been the main employers of teachers since the last decades of the nineteenth century when teaching and teachers in elementary schools were

76

still struggling to establish some kind of status in the community. There has been very little apparent feeling of identity between teachers in local authority primary and secondary schools, the older grammar schools, private preparatory and the great public schools and even less between them and those teaching in technical colleges and universities. The result has been a number of professional associations catering for sectional interests, although recently there have been efforts towards a more united front particularly on the part of the National Union of Teachers which is by far the largest professional body in the educational field. This movement towards greater professional unity may be stimulated in part by the apparent necessity to develop a strong negotiating body now that more teachers are affected in some measure by government policy such as the reorganisation of secondary education on comprehensive lines. Although local education committees are statutorily required to have teaching representatives as co-opted members, the teaching profession has never played the same dominant role in the framing of educational policy and its implementation as professional medical organisations have in the National Health Service. Traditionally, it is true, the chief education officer of a local authority has been someone with teaching experience and qualifications but educational administration has tended to develop into a separate specialism of its own. Nevertheless teachers, particularly head teachers, have great freedom in the way they organise their classes, the syllabus they follow and the educational methods they use, although the pressure of external examinations affects this freedom to some extent.

The use of members of the nursing profession in the implementation of social policy shows some marked contrasts. Many of those who work in the domiciliary health services, in the school health service and in industrial health units have the opportunity of using initiative. They may carry a considerable amount of individual responsibility and use their professional knowledge and skill with a minimum amount of supervision. Those in the hospital service however still tend to work in a clearly defined and often rigid hierarchy of authority. Most residential institutions show complex administrative patterns and difficult staffing problems. They merit special consideration although a very brief one in this survey.

Residential institutions

Despite the current emphasis on 'community care', the development of social policy has also led to a greater interest recently in the quality of our provision of residential institutions. The increasing population, particularly the increase in the number of older people, the rise in the crime rate, the new attitude to mental illness are all factors which have encouraged this new look at institutional care and treatment. There is of course a very great variety of such institutions and because they serve a number of functions they show very different patterns of organisation and administration. Some, such as children's homes and residential accommodation for the elderly and infirm, are primarily concerned with providing a good substitute for a family home; some children however may be so emotionally and socially damaged that they require residential care in a 'therapeutic community' where active treatment may also be involved. Many penal establishments are seen today as having triple goals not easily reconciled—protecting the public by keeping criminals in custody, providing a deterrent to would-be law-breakers, and reforming the prisoner. The problems resulting from the attempt to use a prison sentence as a means of rehabilitation are, for example, indicated in a study of an American prison camp made by Oscar Grusky (1959). This study suggests that the introduction of new aims and

78

methods of treatment in an institution will bring many consequential changes in organisation, in relationships and procedures.

A study of certain hospital administrators concluded that the group secretary was primarily a group communications officer; as secretary to the management committee he put into effect committee decisions through minutes, letters and memoranda. The hospital secretary was a co-ordination and liaison officer who put people in touch with one another. The matron was primarily a 'departmental head directing the various domestic and nursing departments under her control and her activities did not usually require previous committee approval' (from 'A Study of Six Hospital Administrators' by R. B. Adcock and others reported in *The Hospital*, June 1966. Although this study was on too small a scale to permit any valid generalisations, yet the results raise interesting points for further study.).

Cartwright (1964) found that one of the greatest problems in hospital was caused by the failure to recognise patients' social and psychological requirements.

The hospital becomes inevitably—and in a sense rightly—more bureaucratic; responsibilities are defined and divided and arrangements are made for the regular and continuous fulfilment of these duties. This has happened for the physical care of patients. But in many hospitals no comparable systematic arrangements have been introduced for giving patients information. . . . Explanations need to be seen not as a lavish appendage, but as an integral part of medical care. Recognition and acceptance of this responsibility could stimulate interest in patients' social lives, so that hospital staff become more aware of the difficulties patients may encounter when they leave hospital. This in turn could lead to greater integration between hospital and welfare services and between hospital and general practitioner.

These brief comments may serve to suggest that residential institutions as instruments of social policy raise a number of problems. Firstly by definition, residential institutions provide shelter in addition to serving some other purpose for their residents or for society. Thus boarding schools provide education, hospitals treatment, prisons safe custody in addition to shelter. In varying degrees the individual in the institution has to pursue his domestic, work and leisure activities within a circumscribed area, within what Goffman (1962) calls the 'total institution'. This tendency towards exclusiveness necessarily limits the freedom of choice of the individual and, because he has to play all his social roles within a limited environment, his experience may tend to be restrictive and frustrating to a much greater degree than if he were living a more 'normal' life in his own home. A maximum security prison is likely to provide the most restrictive form of experience; in other institutions such as a hostel for adolescent boys this 'inclusiveness' may scarcely exist at all, and it may have very little significance for those who are seriously ill in hospital or otherwise incapacitated and unable to cope with a less sheltered environment. Within the institution consideration must be given to ensure that as much real freedom of choice as possible is seen as the *right* of every resident—which incidentally may sometimes be easier to achieve in larger than in smaller institutions.

Secondly, the recent emphasis on community care in the social services has had many good results, but it has tended to discount the positive value of much residential care and treatment and has increased the stigma felt by some residents and accentuated the feeling of 'difference' which residing in a Home or other form of institution would seem to develop. This is of course not true of all forms of institutional care or treatment; for instance the demand for beds in maternity wards appears to be rising rapidly! But in residential Homes, in psychiatric hospitals and in a number of penal institutions a sense of failure is apparent in both residents and staff for so often institutional care is seen as a 'last resort'—to be used when all else fails. On the other hand the attempt in some places to make institutional care or treatment a vital part of total *community care* has resulted from a new understanding of the positive part which institutions can and do play in modern society. The old rigid distinction between 'institution' and 'community' is beginning to be blurred by such developments as day-hospitals, hostels, arrangements whereby in-patients go out to local firms to work, occupation and training centres and other forms of community provision. Similarly there is beginning to be some breaking down of the rigid classification of institutions according to administrative and statutory criteria, a classification which has often meant that the needs of individuals have not been met because they did not comply with certain of the eligibility requirements of the institution which in all other ways was most appropriate for them. Thus the Mental Health Act, 1959 made it possible for hospital accommodation to be used more flexibly to meet the needs of psychiatric patients, and recent changes in the law relating to the treatment of offenders has also meant that a much wider variety of institutions can be used for their rehabilitation. But much remains to be done.

Within institutions another factor which can cause problems is what Goffman has termed the 'binary' system; members of the institution are divided into two distinct groups, the managers and the managed, the teachers and the taught, the medical staff and patients, the officers and the prisoners. In many situations this division may be accentuated by a conscious widening of social distance between the two, often as a help to maintain discipline and control as in prison. An inappropriate emphasis or use of this difference may hinder the attainment of the aims of the institution, a point which is being emphasised by those who are exploring the concept of the 'therapeutic community'.

Fourthly, a major problem in many institutions is that of staff. Just because of the 'inclusive' nature of much of the life in residential work, it does not always attract enough staff of the appropriate calibre. It is only recently that there has been much interest in the organisational structure and dynamics of residential institutions and very little help in the way of training has been available for recruits. Many of those working in institutions, whether resident or non-resident, are of course highly trained specialists in their own profession or occupation, but this has not necessarily prepared them in any helpful way for the peculiar problems of the environment in which they will work. There is increasing interest in the whole problem of residential staff and new forms of training are being studied and discussed as in *Caring for People* (1967) the Report of the expert committee of enquiry set up by the National Council of Social Service under the chairmanship of Lady Williams. A significant development has taken place in recent years which may have far-reaching effect on many institutions and that is the increasing use of non-resident staff—in hospitals, in children's homes and other forms of residential care.

Finally, many institutions today are large, complex organisations and as indicated above, require the use of modern management techniques for the function of the institution to be carried out efficiently. There is increasing interest in this as a field of study and practice, and, for instance, hospital administration is being seen more and more as a specialised profession in its own right. At present there is too little knowledge of whether the sophisticated techniques of modern management which appear to be successful in industry are applicable in total or in part to service organisations and particularly to residential institutions.

Decision-making and the citizen

Decisions made at all levels within the social services directly and indirectly affect the lives of millions of people. While many of these decisions are comparatively routine, others may be of an extremely fateful nature for the person about whom they are made. As Keith-Lucas (1957) has pointed out 'They may mean, in effect, the difference between health and sickness, between dependence and independence, between continuance or severing of family ties between misery and well-being, and, it is not too much to suggest, on occasion, between life and death itself'. We said earlier that one of the aims of contemporary social policy is sometimes seen as giving people a greater degree of choice. For many of the poorer and more vulnerable members of society, the degree of independence and freedom of action accepted as a right by the more affluent was in the past, and still is, a mirage. That greater freedom of choice should become a reality for them depends not only on the improvement of social and economic conditions but also on the innumerable decisions taken by many officials and other workers concerned with the implementation of social policy. Ginsberg (1965) in discussing the right to education considers that

> The duty of the state is to ensure that all its future citizens are given the opportunity of acquiring that degree of education which will enable them to make an intelligent decision as to their own capacities or potentialities and provide the basis for the knowledge and discipline needed for active participation in the work and collective decisions of the community.

For this opportunity to be an actuality for *all* children

83

depends to a large extent on the understanding, knowledge and skill of those engaged in the administrative process necessary to provide schools and educational equipment as well as the teachers on whom the immediate responsibility falls. So too with the other social rights of the citizen today. Administrative process and personnel are as important as policy if these rights are to be realities.

6

Social policy and national resources

The implementation of social policy is always governed by the availability of appropriate resources. These include land, buildings and a variety of material equipment but ultimately the major factors which have to be considered are manpower and finance. To some extent the number of people employed will depend upon the money available to pay them but two additional factors have to be taken into consideration: the size of the total labour force, actual and potential, in the country, and the number of people within this total capable of being trained to carry out the highly technical and skilled jobs required in some services. Similarly financial resources available depend first on the total national product and only secondly on the percentage of this which the public is prepared to devote to meeting social need through taxation, insurance contributions, or consumer payments. We shall consider each of these two main factors, manpower and financial resources, in turn.

Problems of manpower

An early concern of the state was in the control of those

occupations where it was considered that members of the public were particularly vulnerable. For at least five centuries there has been some regulation and protection of the legal profession, an occupation whose ability and integrity is closely bound up with the administration of justice. As far back as the thirteenth century it was laid down that no man was to exercise openly the 'office of advocation' without three years' 'good study of Canon Law and Civil Law', and since 1729 every candidate for admission as a solicitor or attorney has been required to have been articled. Under the Solicitors Act, 1843, the Law Society, a voluntary organisation of qualified and registered solicitors, was appointed registrar, or custodian, of the Roll of solicitors. Both the Law Society and the Bar Council, representing barristers, have important statutory duties under the Legal Aid and Advice Acts and their members have statutorily recognised monopolies of certain appointments and of drafting conveyances and other legal documents.

The nineteenth and twentieth centuries have seen the emergence of other professions which have obtained legal recognition entailing a certain monopoly of practice in the interests of the public. It was in the nineteenth century that the medical profession obtained a distinctive legal status. The Medical Act, 1858, created the General Council of Medical Education and Registration of the United Kingdom to regulate the conditions under which candidates could enter the medical profession and to register those who qualified. This Act was followed by a long series of Acts which have sought to ensure at least a minimum standard of training and practice in this and other occupations through the setting up of professional councils to approve training courses and maintain registers. Examples of such acts are the Dentists Acts of 1878, 1921 and 1952, the Nurses Registration Act, 1919, the Nurses Acts, 1943, 1949, the Midwives Acts, 1902, 1918 and 1936. Statutory action of this kind has strengthened and confirmed control of these professions by their own members although the details of regulation have varied. Much of the actual training and education has been left to independent bodies such as university medical schools, but nursing and midwifery training schools became an integral part of the National Health Service after the Act of 1946.

As soon as the state accepts responsibility for providing certain services, it has to concern itself with the recruitment of sufficient workers of the right calibre and training to man them. This concern increases as the concept of 'social rights' emerges. If there is the implication that every child has the right to receive education suited to his age, aptitude and ability, and every citizen the right to appropriate medical care, then some person or organisation has the duty of ensuring that there are enough teachers, doctors, nurses and other medical and educational personnel to meet the demand so that these rights may be effectively exercised. It follows therefore that the state becomes involved in the recruitment and training of many different kinds of personnel and is concerned with both quantitative and qualitative problems.

In the Civil Service itself about one in ten of the non-industrial staff is employed in the social service departments. Most of these belong to the ordinary, clerical, executive and administrative grades of staff but some are specialists with professional qualifications. The service nature of the Ministry of Social Security means that this department employs more than half of these, between 50-60,000 in 1966. Some two-thirds of the 16,100 employed in the Home Office are in the Prison Department concerned with the administration and staffing of all our penal establishments; it is a debatable point whether all, or any, of these should be included in a count of 'social service' personnel.

In all the local authority social services there is a shortage of trained staff and if, as seems inevitable, the demand on the services continues to grow, a considerable increase in recruitment must be faced in the near future. For example, Paige and Jones in their study of the Health and Welfare Services in 1975 for the National Institute of Economic and Social Research estimate that the total staff in these services (including school health and child care) in 1960 was 594,600 and that there must be an increase of 44% in manpower between 1960 and 1975. They go on to suggest that as the total national labour force is only expected to increase by about six per cent, this will mean a rise in the proportion employed in the health and welfare services. They consider that 'Such a rise is to be expected, however, in a period of faster economic growth, and it will be made possible by rising productivity in the industrial sectors. A bigger problem is to meet the requirements for trained professional staff.'

The same kind of trend and a similar problem are to be found in the education service. The number of teachers in primary and secondary schools in England and Wales in 1965 was 330,367, but the number of pupils in these schools, including those staying beyond the statutory leaving age, is expected to increase by about eleven per cent in the early nineteen-seventies. The number of people required to teach them will be an additional 62,000 if some improvement in staffing standards is allowed for and if the raising of the school leaving age in 1970-71 is taken into account.

Evidence for the increasing involvement by the state in the recruitment and training of workers in the developing services is seen in the long list of committees set up by successive governments to consider manpower needs. Examples are: The Working Party on the Recruitment and Training of Nurses, 1947; the Committee on the Supply, Recruitment and Training of Teachers and Youth Leaders, 1944; the Committee on Medical Auxiliaries, 1951; the

Committee on Recruitment to the Dental Profession, 1956; An Inquiry into Health Visiting: the Working Party on the Field of Work, Training and Recruitment of Health Visitors, 1956; the Committee to consider the Future Numbers of Medical Practitioners and the Appropriate Intake of Medical Students, 1957; the Working Party on Social Workers in the Local Authority Health and Welfare Services, 1959; the Committee on the Youth Service, 1960; the Departmental Committee on the Probation Service, 1962.

The result of these and similar inquiries has been varied. For instance in the case of nursing the need to stimulate recruitment both during the war and after led to the setting up of a special branch within the Ministry of Labour in 1943, and the establishment of Nursing Appointment Officers throughout the country. The increasing demand for teachers has led to a rapid expansion of training facilities and to an energetic campaign undertaken jointly by local authorities and the Department of Education and Science to attract married women back into the schools. The Treasury has made money available for the expansion of existing medical schools and the establishment of new ones. As a result of the Report of the Care of Children Committee, the Home Office set up a Central Training Council in Child Care in 1947; the Albemarle Report on the Youth Service led to the establishment of the National College for Youth Leaders. Inevitably problems of training and problems of recruitment go hand in hand, but there are some significant differences in the extent and method of government involvement in meeting these problems and in the part played by professional organisations.

Although the state made increasing use of members of the medical and nursing professions in the early decades of this century, it is only since the inauguration of the National Health Service that it has become the largest employer, that is *after* these occupations had become established as self-regulated and controlled professions. Thus while seeking to recruit an adequate supply of doctors, dentists and nurses to meet rising demands, and to discharge its responsibility to provide a comprehensive service to all who may need it, the state is under pressure from the professional organisations to maintain standards of training and entry into these occupations. Because of the long training period involved the present shortage of doctors and dentists cannot be overcome quickly. Crash-training programmes are not acceptable to the professions, nor indeed to the prospective patients, and thus if the situation is to be eased, increasing attention will have to be paid to the deployment of doctors and dentists, and to the use of ancillary staff.

Advances in medical science have led to increased specialisms within the medical profession itself and to the development of a number of ancillary professions such as radiography, physiotherapy and occupational therapy. Although the Cope Committee, set up by the Ministry of Health to review the recruitment, training and qualifications of medical auxiliaries, reported in 1951, it was not until 1960 that the Professions Supplementary to Medicine Act was passed. This provided for a Council with specialist boards for the registration of chiropodists, dieticians, medical laboratory technicians, occupational therapists, physiotherapists, radiographers and remedial gymnasts. The General Medical Council and the General Nursing Council are both dominated by members of the respective professions, but the Council for Professions Supplementary to Medicine is made up in almost equal proportions of representatives of the specialist boards, medical practitioners and lay persons appointed by the Privy Council and the government departments concerned. The composition of the Council and of its specialist Boards illustrates both the ancillary nature of these occupations and the new interest of government departments in the recruitment and training of the workers necessary for the staffing of the health services.

This new interest is also seen in the developments that have taken place in the last three decades in the recruitment, training and employment of social workers in the statutory services. Unlike medical practitioners and nurses, social workers have experienced the growth of professional organisation concurrently with the development of statutory employment. As early as 1907, a Hospital Almoners' Council was formed to be responsible for recruiting and training almoners. Since 1945 the Institute of Almoners (now the Institute of Medical Social Workers) has carried out the function of both a professional organisation and a training body. Since 1945 although the Association of Psychiatric Social Workers (first founded in 1929) has not itself been responsible for professional training it has influenced the content and organisation of university courses in mental health and psychiatric social work. There does not seem to have been any great sense of urgency on the part of the Government, however, to provide a comprehensive coverage of medical social workers and psychiatric social workers in hospitals during the past two or three decades. The Cope Committee reporting in 1951 estimated that about 2,500 to 3,000 almoners would be needed to provide a full hospital service in England and Wales and about 500 in Scotland. The Mackintosh Committee reporting in 1951 estimated that the demand for psychiatric social workers in hospital was at least 800 in addition to some 500 needed for child guidance and 200 for the aftercare services of local health authorities. At that date there were only 331 qualified psychiatric social workers in posts in the United Kingdom. By 1965 only 821 medical social workers and 220 psychiatric social workers were in hospital posts although some of the deficiency has been met by the use of untrained or differently trained workers.

The situation has been quite different in the Probation

and Child-Care Services, where the Home Office has been concerned to ensure a great increase in the number of trained probation and child care officers. Evidence of this concern is seen in the existence of the Training Committee of the Advisory Council for Probation and After-Care and the Central Training Council in Child Care, both under the direct control of the Home Office. Their function is to stimulate recruitment and the provision of training facilities for the staff of the probation service and of local authority children's departments respectively and funds are available specifically for these purposes. Because of the rapid development of the services there is a danger that the quality of new recruits and standards of training may be sacrificed to quantity in view of the pressure to man them. Although the Probation and After-Care Training Committee, like the Central Training Council in Child Care, recognises those who successfully complete social work training courses provided by the universities, and has been instrumental in setting-up some of these, the greatest number of probation officers are trained in courses for which the Home Office, mainly through its inspectorate, are directly responsible. Both Councils are appointed by the Secretary of State. About half the members of the Central Training Council come from local government, others come mainly from voluntary organisations, universities and government departments. The Advisory Council for Probation and After-Care consists of sixteen members including two principal probation officers: its Training Committee is composed of all the members of the Council and fourteen additional members having special knowledge and experience of training for professional social work. In 1966 there were only two serving probation officers and an additional principal probation officer. It is interesting to compare this with the composition of the Councils regulating education and training in the older professions. In any case responsibility for the training scheme and the selection of the

92

majority of students remains with the Home Office Inspectorate.

It was perhaps because of criticisms based on the inappropriateness of a government department discharging in this way its responsibilities for training workers laying claim to professional status, that the Working Party on Social Workers in the Local Authority Health and Welfare Departments proposed the setting up of a Training Council for Social Workers which would have some measure of autonomy. The Council for Training in Social Work (limited at present to social work in the health and welfare services), together with the Council for the Training of Health Visitors, was established under the Health Visiting and Social Work (Training) Act, 1962. This Act makes provision for the Privy Council to appoint one person to be chairman of both these Councils. Of the other thirty-two members of the Council for Training in Social Work, ten are appointed by local authorities, fourteen by the Health Ministers (of which ten must be appointed after consultation with organisations representing social workers or otherwise concerned with social work, and two after consultation with the British Medical Association and the Society of Medical Officers of Health) and seven by the Health Ministers and the Minister of Education after consultation with universities and other educational bodies. The composition of the Council for the Training of Health Visitors is determined by the Act and is on similar lines. These Councils are statutorily charged with the responsibility for promoting training in health visiting and social work, for approving courses and for conducting examinations and thus have a vital part to play in ensuring an adequate supply of suitable personnel for the health and welfare services.

A number of questions are raised by this development and by the implementation of the Professions Supplementary to Medicine Act. Should the relevant central government departments be responsible for professional training and if so, what should be the extent of their responsibility? What part should employing bodies such as the local authorities play? Should representatives of other professional groups be members of training councils by statute? If so, should this pattern be extended to the older professions and their training and registration councils include members of other professions, and of employing and consumer interests? (Proposals are at present under consideration for the reorganisation of the General Nursing Council on these lines.) A number of significant points were made about the powers of central and local government bodies over training in the debates in the House of Commons on the Health Visiting and Social Work (Training) Bill in 1961.

One of the problems in the growth of social work as a professional activity has been the way in which social workers have been divided according to administrative convenience rather than according to specialisation of knowledge and skills. Professional organisations have tended to follow these administrative divisions but in recent years there has been a movement towards greater unification. The formation of a Standing Conference of Organisations of Social Workers in 1962 may be the forerunner of a unified professional organisation. In the universities which have provided training courses for social workers, there has been a strong movement towards forms of 'generic' training which are seen as more appropriate for vocational education at university level, and a measure of agreement has been reached with the government departments concerned with the training for social workers that 'generically' trained students may, with some safeguards, be recognised as trained for their specialist services. In view of the changes taking place at present in the organisation of the social services as well as of the social work profession it would be surprising if considerable changes were

94

not to take place in the organisation of training in the near future. The problem of reconciling quantity and quality still remains.

The report of the Working Party on Social Workers in Local Authority Health and Welfare Services (1959) suggested that a new type of ancillary worker should be recruited, the welfare assistant, who although not a social worker would be able to undertake a wide range of routine tasks under the supervision of a professionally trained social worker. Most local authorities have taken up this suggestion but the differences in qualification and training of other staff undertaking welfare duties blurs the distinction which the Working Party considered should be maintained between such assistants and the qualified social worker. It remains to be seen whether the present developments will, as some people fear, devalue the status of professional social work and lead to a lowering of the standard of competence of the worker deemed to be trained.

Similar fears have been expressed by members of the teaching profession, who have sought to draw a distinction between the ancillary worker, that is a teacher's assistant whose duties should be those determined by the qualified teacher to whom the helper is responsible, and the auxiliary, that is an assistant teacher. It is the latter who are particularly seen as a threat to standards and the professional organisations of teachers also fear that teachers' assistants might be accepted by local authorities in a time of acute shortage as assistant teachers just as an apprentice who serves his time emerges as a craftsman. An ancillary worker is seen as always working under the direction of the trained teacher, who retains overall responsibility for work done in the classroom.

The history of the relationship of the teaching profession with the government has in any case been a curious one. The first government subsidies in the field of education were given towards the training of teachers. The government inspectorate for a long time played a most important part in raising the standard of teaching and indeed in arrangements for the admission of students to training colleges, their instruction and examination and in the award of their final qualification to teach. The Committee appointed in 1942 by the President of the Board of Education to consider the supply, recruitment and training of teachers and youth leaders recommended that the government should withdraw from its previous very close association with teacher training, and the major responsibility for the maintenance and improvement of standards in this field was subsequently given to University Institutes of Education. Recently there have been demands by many members of the teaching organisations that a Teachers' Council should be set up on lines similar to that of the General Medical Council, but so far the government has not agreed that this is desirable.

A summary of problems of supply and training

Thus a number of problems affecting the supply and use of trained manpower for the social services can be identified and may be described briefly:

1. There is the need to increase the numbers of people in the established professions to meet rising demand. This is complicated by the increase in scientific knowledge and the necessity of making professional education both comprehensive and responsive to contemporary conditions. Thus it is necessary not only to expand the numbers of doctors but to ensure that their training is relevant to the needs of modern society and takes account of the rapidly increasing body of scientific knowledge.

2. Partly because of the resulting higher standards of attainment expected of such practitioners, partly because of the impossibility of any one individual being

able to comprehend the amount of knowledge available, specialisation becomes inevitable with the consequence that a more complex organisation of service is required to co-ordinate the work of the practitioners. Thus problems of administration arise and with them a demand for professional training for such administrators.

3. As, however, it is often impossible to recruit a sufficient number of trainees of a sufficient calibre to undergo the necessary education, groups of ancillary workers may spring up. Decisions have to be taken determining what procedures or forms of help can be undertaken by less well-qualified staff. This development may again lead to problems of deployment and the relationship of these new workers to each other and to the older professional groups, for instance, the relationship of members of the professions supplementary to medicine to doctors, and to nurses.

4. There is a demand for new types of worker, and also for the training of workers in posts who were recruited when the concept of their job was very different from that of today. For example there is a demand for highly trained child-care officers to work in the children's service, for trained mental welfare officers in mental health departments and for training facilities to be made available for experienced but unqualified workers.

Because of the growth of the concept of the social rights of the citizen, the government is under pressure to man certain services adequately, employing officers with as much training as finance and training resources allow. Thus probation committees are under a duty to provide sufficient probation officers as the needs of the courts require. A public scandal will ensue if a child is not removed from surroundings which are harmful to him through the insufficiency of child-care officers. The danger of lowering standards of competence in order to achieve comprehen-

97

sive coverage is seen by many people to be at the heart of the problem of staffing in all the public social services. In any case, care must be taken to ensure the best deployment of scarce resources through good management and the use of all appropriate forms of labour-saving equipment.

Financial resources

In the first chapter we suggested that social policy in any state is vitally affected by the economic conditions of the society concerned. The comparative affluence or poverty of the society will affect the priorities given to certain courses of action and will be one of the main factors in determining the amount of national income which can be spent on social action and services. The hope which is sometimes expressed that as society becomes more affluent the amount spent on the social services will diminish both relatively and absolutely appears to be a vain one. It is not only that higher standards of expectation rise with the growing affluence of the population of any country, but that the *pattern* of expectation seems to vary from country to country even where similar economic conditions exist. An indication of this is seen in the differing amounts of the gross national product spent on social security, health services and education in the countries of Western Europe. A further illustration can be seen by a comparison of the quantity of housing available and the differences in equipment from country to country discussed by Donnison (1967) in *The Government of Housing*.

In this country there has been a steady rise in the percentage of the gross national product at factor cost spent on the social services: from 13·7% in 1950 to 18·1% in 1965 (see Table I). Table II gives the expenditure on services officially classed as 'social services' while Table III gives expenditure on certain other types of relevant public

98

TABLE I

Public Expenditure as % of G.N.P. (Gross National Product)

Type of Service	1955 %	1965 %
1. Military Service	9.05	6.76
2. Civil Service	0.18	0.08
3. External Relations	0.80	0.97
4. Roads & Public Lighting	0.80	1.38
5. Transport & Communication	1.28	1.86
6. Employment Services	0.15	0.14
7. Other Industry & Trade	2.85	3.27
8. Research	0.20	0.50
9. Agriculture, Forestry & Food	1.11	1.08
10. Housing	3.13	3.02
11. Water, Sewage & Refuse	0.69	0.82
12. Public Health Services	0.08	0.11
13. Land Drainage & Coast Protection	0.09	0.08
14. Parks, Pleasure Grounds, etc.	0.16	0.22
15. Miscellaneous Environment Services	0.39	0.56
16. Libraries, Museums & Arts	0.10	0.16
17. Police	0.54	0.68
18. Prisons	0.06	0.12
19. Parliament & Law Courts	0.10	0.15
20. Fire Service	0.14	0.17
21. Education	3.23	5.06
22. National Health Service	3.41	4.10
23. Local Welfare Services	0.11	0.18
24. Child Care	0.12	0.14
25. School Meals, Milk & Welfare Food	0.48	0.42
26. Social Security	5.85	7.79
27. Finance & Tax-Collection	0.58	0.50
28. Other Services	0.74	0.34
Total public expenditure	36.42	40.69

N.B. Items 21-26 inclusive are officially classified as Social Services. (Based on statistics from *National Income and Expenditure*, H.M.S.O.)

TABLE II

Public Expenditure on the Social Services 1955-65

£ million

	1955	1956	1957	1958	1959	1960	1961	1962	1963	1964	1965
Education	549	636	727	779	847	916	1,012	1,172	1,281	1,410	1,567
National Health Service	579	633	685	728	788	861	930	971	1,035	1,126	1,269
Local welfare services	19	21	24	25	28	32	37	43	47	54	57
Child care	21	22	23	25	25	26	29	32	35	38	43
School meals, milk & welfare foods	82	89	85	79	83	86	93	99	105	115	130
National insurance, pensions and assistance	993	1,062	1,117	1,345	1,450	1,488	1,628	1,744	1,988	2,097	2,413
Total social services	2,243	2,463	2,661	2,982	3,221	3,409	3,729	4,061	4,491	4,840	5,479

(Source: National Income and Expenditure, H.M.S.O.)

provision. From the figures in Tables II and III it can be seen that the greatest expenditure is on insurance, pensions and assistance, while environmental services, education and the National Health Service take roughly equal amounts from public funds. All of these services are of direct benefit to the majority of the population—at least at some time in their lives. Those services which are primarily concerned with providing social work help and other forms of social welfare, such as child-care and the local welfare services, account for a very small proportion of the national expenditure—some 0·4% of the gross national product in 1965.

The largest single item of expenditure of local authorities is the provision of education; this service accounted for one-third of the total expenditure of local authorities in 1954/55, rising to one-half in 1963/65. The second major item of expenditure is that on housing but the greater part of the current expenditure on housing by local authorities is covered by the income from rents, amounting, for instance, to £289,500,000 for all authorities in 1963/64, and to £329,500,000 in 1965/66.

If we go on to consider further the methods by which public expenditure, both centrally and locally, is financed, a number of interesting points may be noted. First, although most of the expenditure on the social services comes from central government funds the income the Exchequer receives from other resources including taxation on expenditure (that is indirect taxation) is greater than that from taxation on income (see Table IV). This means that it is difficult to do any simple calculations about The net effect of taxation and social benefits in the case of individuals. Attempts have been made to estimate the effect of taxation, both direct and indirect, on the one hand, and of all social benefits on the other for individuals and families in different income groups. The results are given in *Economic Trends* for 1962, 1964 and 1966 published by

TABLE III

Expenditure on certain other Public Services, 1955-65

£ million

	1955	1956	1957	1958	1959	1960	1961	1962	1963	1964	1965
Employment services	25	26	27	28	29	31	31	32	34	36	43
Housing	532	497	470	420	442	496	564	530	601	808	934
Water, sewerage and refuse disposal	117	129	133	141	155	165	187	209	217	242	255
Public health services	14	16	17	18	19	21	24	26	28	31	34
Parks, pleasure grounds, etc.	27	30	33	35	38	43	48	54	57	62	68
Libraries, museums and arts	17	19	22	25	26	30	34	38	41	45	50

(Source: National Income and Expenditure, H.M.S.O.)

the Central Statistical Office. These calculations are based on a very small sample and involve a good many assumptions and approximations. They take no account of the proportion of taxation paid by such individuals and families which goes towards other public expenditure such as that on defence or the maintenance of law and order.

Secondly, the contribution made by the Exchequer from taxation to the cost of social security has been increasing

TABLE IV

Receipts of Central Government

	1955 %	1965 %
Gross Trading Income	1·4	0·2
Rent, Dividends & Interest	4·6	6·7
Taxes on Income	42·8	39·5
Taxes on Expenditure	40·2	37·0
National Insurance & Health Contributions	10·0	16·6
Total ...	100·0	100·0
Amount in £ millions ...	5,465	10,182

Receipts of Local Authorities

	1955 %	1965 %
Gross Trading Income	2·8	2·3
Rent, Dividends & Interest	17·4	18·4
Rates	39·3	39·3
Current Grants from Central Government	40·5	40·0
Total ...	100·0	100·0
Amount in £ millions ...	1,121	3,128

(Source: *National Income and Expenditure*, H.M.S.O.)

steadily and accounts for a larger share of the revenue of the National Insurance Fund. Thus in 1957/58 the total receipts of the National Insurance Fund amounted to £1,119,606,000 of which £103,150,000 was contributed from the Exchequer through Parliamentary vote; the comparable figures for 1964/65 were £1,705,481,000 and £224,105,000. The fact that this subvention has had to be increased is one indication that 'social insurance' is moving further away from the basic principles of insurance. Indeed, it is considered by some people to be merely a convenient way of raising money and giving insured persons a 'right' to assistance without the operation of a means test.

Thirdly, the amount of the national health contribution made by employers and insured persons, providing some 13% of the expenditure on the National Health Service in 1965/66, has risen twice as much as other forms of national income between 1955 and 1965. It is difficult to see a justification for this contribution except an historic one; the health service is not based on insurance principles and the contribution is a form of regressive taxation.

Fourthly, the contribution from local rates is still an important item in providing funds for the social services. Thus in 1963/64 the income from rates in England and Wales was £923,077,000 whereas government grants to local authorities totalled £1,022,446,000, the ratio remaining almost the same between 1955/65.

Unless there are radical changes in social policy in the near future, expenditure on the social services is likely to continue to rise. Paige and Jones (1966), for instance, estimate that a total increase of about 54% in the volume of current expenditure on the National Health Service between 1960 and 1975 will be necessary to meet the needs of population increase, to provide for higher standards within the service corresponding to the rise expected in the country as a whole and to make good some of the existing deficiencies. The Government's National Plan published in 1965 provided for an increase of 23½% in the five-year period to 1970 in the National Health Service and certain related expenditure. The main elements in this increase were for the continued development of the Hospital Service, both new hospitals and the improvement of services within the hospitals; the improvement of conditions of general practitioners and a very rapid growth of local authority health services (see Table V).

Similarly, expenditure under the heading of education would increase by 32% in real terms from 1964/65 to 1969/70. If productivity were to rise as expected in the Plan much of this increase in expenditure would be met by the rise in the gross national product without the need to increase taxation. If, however, as seems likely, the hoped-for increase in productivity is not attained then difficult decisions will have to be made about priorities. It is a question not only of whether greater resources should be spent on education than on health, housing or other services but of how consumption is divided between the public and private sector.

In earlier chapters we discussed the way in which both business concerns and mutual-benefit organisations are used to carry out some aspects of social policy and recently it has been argued by a group of economists that the whole basis of our social provision should be reconsidered. It is suggested that most of our schools, medical care and insurance cover should be provided by private enterprise and the individual left to make his own arrangements to meet his needs. Those in financial difficulty would receive help, possibly in the form of vouchers which they would be able to use to 'buy' the education, medical care or insurance cover which they and their dependents required. Arthur Seldon suggests that

A wider choice by tax rebates or vouchers would enlarge

TABLE V

Public Expenditure by Function[1]

£ million, 1965 Survey prices

	1964/65[3]	1965/66[4]	1969/70
	1964 Survey estimates	1965 Survey estimates	
Main programmes:			
Defence Budget	2,073	2,134	2,075
Roads	406	426	575
Public Housing Investment	519	571	691
Housing subsidies, etc. ...	153	164	257
Police and prisons ...	230	237	281
Education (with school meals and milk) ...	1,459	1,574	1,923
Health and welfare (with welfare foods)	1,238	1,316	1,529
Benefits and assistance (with family allowances)	2,120	2,379	2,920
Total	8,198	8,801	10,251
Other programmes	2,602	2,775	2,994
Contingency allowance ...	—	—	100
Total[2]	10,800	11,576[5]	13,295

(Source: *The National Plan 1965* H.M.S.O.)

[1] The expenditure shown for each function is that of Great Britain spending authorities.

[2] This total relates to public expenditure as defined in paragraph 1 above. It is the same as the total in Table 48 of the *National Income Blue Book* and in the table at the back of the Blue Book called *Treasury Analysis of Public Expenditure*, except for the exclusion of the investment of nationalised industries, etc. This is the total which the Government decided to contain within an average increase of $4\frac{1}{4}\%$ a year at constant prices in the period 1964/65 to 1969/70.

[3] These are estimates for 1964/65 made for the Government's first analysis from which the '$4\frac{1}{4}\%$' decision was taken, adjusted to 1965 Survey prices (see note 4).

[4] Estimates of summer 1965 at prices related to the Budget Estimates of 1965/66. These prices are used for the 1969/70 figures also and are called '1965 Survey prices'.

[5] This total does not take account of the measures announced by the Govt. on 27th July 1965, the effect of which can be expected to be a reduction in the order of £100 million in 1965/66.

the resources of manpower and capital invested in education, health services, housing and pensions. . . . We should also put more resources into welfare if we paid for individual services by fees or insurance than if we continued to buy standardized services from the state and paid for them by taxation.

If the provision of 'welfare' by private enterprise is encouraged instead of discouraged by government policy then Seldon sees the coming of a welfare utopia instead of a welfare state; 'Welfare expenditure as a percentage of national income could rise substantially and quickly without fuss, without inflation, without enmeshing welfare in party politics, national finance or balance of payments crises' If this argument is valid it is perhaps surprising that in a time of rising affluence for many individuals, private expenditure accounted for a smaller proportion of the total expenditure on health provision in 1962 than in 1951. So far the suggestions put forward for this dismantling of the welfare state have not been accepted as official policy by any political party. It could be that the voucher system still recalls to many the 'relief ticket' characteristic of the Poor Law administration.

Another point of view which has been put forward recently is that the main burden of payment for the social services should be switched from the citizen as a tax-and rate-payer to the citizen as a consumer without the state withdrawing as the main provider of 'welfare'. That is, many services at present provided free to the consumer when needed would be charged for either at full or part cost; those unable to pay the full charge would be subject to an income test. The debate on prescription charges is an illustration of the difference of opinion about this. Although these were abolished in 1965 (but restored in 1968), charges for other parts of the health service brought in nearly £30 million in 1965. Fees are still charged for much higher education and the parents of students are subject to a means test. Arguments for the retention and extension of such charges have been variously based: public money should not be spent on providing people with things they can provide for themselves; such charges prevent the abuse of the services; they provide an additional form of income which is more acceptable to most people than paying taxes or rates. The counter-arguments run: the community has a direct interest in seeing that its members are well-educated, receive medical treatment when necessary, are well-housed and have a reasonable income on which to live; abuse of services can be prevented more efficiently in other ways, whereas income tests often prevent people from taking the help they need or continuing with the education for which they are suitable, thus leading to a waste of human resources and hardship to the individual; the collection of charges and the operation of means tests is a costly administrative operation. In connection with this last argument it is perhaps of interest to note that expenditure on administration as a percentage of the total amount of money disbursed in 1965/66 was 3·1 for family allowances, 3·5 for national insurance benefits and 8·9 for national assistance. It would be useful to know the cost of collecting prescription charges when these were made if the time of the pharmacists, the civil servants employed by the National Assistance Board, the Ministry of Health and the Executive Councils as well as of the general public concerned could have been estimated with any accuracy. Because of the reluctance already noted towards paying general taxes and rates and because insurance contributions bear more hardly on the poorer members of the community, it has been suggested that our present complex methods of financing the social services should be replaced by a single social security or social service tax, which should be based on ability to pay and which would give entitlement to a whole range of benefits and services. This could simplify some of the complex accounting now necessary but would increase the work of the Commissioners of Inland Revenue and strengthen the social role of this Department. Another limited version of this is the suggestion that family allowances and income tax dependants' allowances should become part of one scheme. Some radical changes in the financing of social policy would seem to be inevitable, but what these changes will be is hard to predict. What is certain is that any changes will be the subject of lively political argument.

Before we leave this subject of finance it must be noted that a considerable sum of money each year is used by the many voluntary organisations. It is estimated that the endowed charitable trusts own in aggregate securities and money worth some £200,000,000 besides a vast amount of land. In addition to contributions from trust funds, voluntary organisations finance their work in a variety of ways, by donations and subscriptions from well-wishers, money-raising events and, as we have mentioned previously, by subsidies from central and local government departments. Moreover the funds of various mutual-aid organisations registered under the Friendly Societies Acts amounted to more than £300,000,000 in 1965.

Thus the pattern of financing the social services and other aspects of social policy is a complex one, giving rise to many problems concerned with decisions about priorities, the distribution of the national income between the public and private sector and the best methods of raising money to finance the former. That so large a proportion of the national income is now devoted to the provision of the social services, both statutory and voluntary, means that all members of the community have a double interest both as taxpayers and as beneficiaries.

7

Co-ordination, confusion and social change

The implementation of social policy, as we have seen, has led to the creation of many organisations and has impinged on numerous others, both in the private and in the public sphere of action. This welter of public and private bodies all affecting in some way the welfare of the individual citizen makes the problem of co-operating a vital one if the needs of all members of the community are to be met efficiently and humanely. Co-operation is a matter of human relationships, involving a willingness on the part of each person to work with others to achieve some end, to provide a service, to meet needs; it can be helped by organisational means, by efficient co-ordinating machinery and by providing conditions of employment which encourage people to work together. The clarification of function of the various departments or organisations involved, the definition of the roles of the workers, good lines of communication to assist the exchange of information and the development of mutual understanding, are all important. The situation is complicated by the rate of change, the necessity of devising new policy and new methods to meet new pressures and new needs, and any devices which are developed in order to facilitate co-operation have to be flexible and under constant reappraisal.

At top level the co-ordinating machinery of the social services is that of the central government itself—through the cabinet, through meetings of ministers, sometimes through the appointment of special ministers (with or without portfolio) with the oversight of several departments; within each department the minister and his senior administrators are responsible for co-ordinating the various branches of that department. At local level, the councils of the counties and county boroughs and their clerks are responsible for the overall co-ordination of the work of the various committees which with their departments are responsible for the specialised work of the councils. There are many devices which have been used to promote co-operation at all levels in the implementation of social policy—inter-departmental committees, cross-representation, special liaison committees, standing or *ad hoc* conferences are examples. In the Health Service for instance, there is cross-representation between Boards of Governors and Regional Hospital Boards, and between Executive Councils and Local Health Authorities. The development of machinery for social and economic planning both nationally and regionally is another example of the way in which the necessity for a team approach is now recognised in this increasingly important field of activity.

The same need for co-ordinating machinery can be seen in the sphere of voluntary action. A number of voluntary organisations aim at bringing together locally and regionally as well as nationally, all those statutory and voluntary bodies and individuals interested in one particular problem or field of activity. Examples of co-ordinating bodies are the Old People's Welfare Committees, the National Association for Mental Health and the Central Council for the Disabled. The Councils of Social Service are unique in that they endeavour to co-ordinate the whole range of welfare activities in a locality in the same way as the National Council of Social Service does for the country as a whole.

It is possible to distinguish at least three kinds of co-ordinating machinery; that which is concerned mainly with planning over a wide range of activities, that which may be said to be 'service' centred and that which is primarily 'client' or 'consumer' centred. The first we have already considered in some detail in an earlier chapter, as in the case of regional social and economic planning. The second endeavours to bring together organisations or departments and is concerned with the development of an agreed policy and the overlap of services as in liaison committees and standing conferences. But there are also co-ordinating committees and case conferences which endeavour to ensure that the resources of the community are used most effectively to meet the needs of individuals or families. Sometimes these operate in a specialised field, such as child guidance or physical rehabilitation, sometimes more generally as in the co-ordinating machinery set up to deal with children neglected in their own homes. For effective co-ordination, the will to co-operate must be there or the co-ordinating body must have the authority to ensure that an agreed common policy is carried out.

A further point to be borne in mind in any discussion of co-ordination is that no machinery will be effective if the services or organisations to be co-ordinated are based on an unrealistic or out-dated division of function. Much of the evidence to the Seebohm Committee set up in 1966 to review local authority personal social services and to make recommendations on their reorganisation, suggests that in spite of co-ordinating machinery and the good will of social workers and local authority officials, many families are not getting effective help; a radical regrouping of the functions of the various departments involved is therefore urged by a number of those submitting evidence to the Committee.

Our analysis of the ways in which social policy is implemented tends to give a picture of administrative confusion. There are broad divisions of function between the various central and local government departments so that, for instance, the Ministry of Health is responsible for seeing that a vast array of medical services are provided; the Department for Education and Science together with the local education authorities provide many different educational institutions; the new Ministry of Social Security is now responsible for meeting financial need arising from many causes. Yet it is the responsibility of the education authorities and not the Ministry of Social Security to provide help in kind in the form of free or partly free school meals where considered necessary, and financial help by the payment of maintenance grants for a wide variety of students; housing authorities are responsible for administering rent-rebate schemes or other forms of subsidised housing to tenants and now local authorities under the Children and Young Persons Act, 1963, have power to assist families in cash or kind. Local health authorities are responsible for health education and the provision of training centres for certain subnormal children and adults, welfare authorities for the home teaching of the blind, and children's committees for approved schools.

In a complex society such as ours, the organisation of resources to meet human need is inevitably a complex operation but it should be possible to prevent some of the overlapping which is present in the administration of our voluntary and statutory services, to fill some of the gaps that occur in our welfare provision and to make more efficient use of available resources of finance and manpower. However, just because social policy is the result of many pressures, vested interests and economic and social factors, social action in the field of welfare appears to be confused, overlapping and ill-co-ordinated. Action which arises from the interest and initiative of individuals and groups tends to be arbitrary, biased, spasmodic and limited as well as creative, concerned and experimental. Moreover the rapidity of social and economic change means that new problems and new needs are constantly arising and new solutions found.

We suggested earlier that social policy and action appears to be affected by four groups of factors: the beliefs, overt and implied, currently held about the nature of man which affect the ends or ultimate goals of action and the values which influence priorities; the beliefs currently held about the function of society and the role of government within it; the contemporary state of scientific knowledge, medical, social and technological; and the economic and social development of the society which will affect standards of living and of expectation. These factors are all mutually interacting and subject to constant change. It is no wonder that at any one time both social policy and the means which are used to implement it give the appearance of confusion and conflict. Any attempt at description and analysis of the means whereby social policy is translated into action must be out of date as soon as it is finished. Yet the attempt must be made. It is only by greater understanding of the forces at work shaping society, the values implicit in social action and the processes involved in meeting the needs of individual citizens that we can hope to respond to the challenge of change.

Suggestions for further reading

Many books have been written about different aspects of social policy and its implementation. Among these the student will find the following particularly useful:

For a discussion of social policy useful books are Kathleen M. Slack, *Social Administration and the Citizen*, Michael Joseph, 1966; T. H. Marshall, *Social Policy*, Heinemann, 1965; D. C. Marsh, *An Introduction to the Study of Social Administration*, Routledge & Kegan Paul, 1965. An interesting historical account of the evolution of social policy under the pressures of war is to be found in R. R. Titmuss, *Problems of Social Policy*, Longmans, 1950. A study of pressure groups and the evolution of social policy in the provision of the health service is given in A. J. Willcocks, *The Creation of the National Health Service*, Routledge & Kegan Paul, 1966.

Discussions of the relationship between voluntary and statutory social services are to be found in M. Rooff's *Voluntary Societies and Social Policy*, Routledge & Kegan Paul, 1957, W. Beveridge's *Voluntary Action*, Allen & Unwin, 1948, as well as in the report of the Committee on the Law and Practice relating to Charitable Trusts (1952) and the periodic reports of the Charity Commission.

A detailed account of the relationship between central and local government is given in J. A. G. Griffiths' *Central Departments and Local Authorities*, Allen & Unwin, 1966. The studies on Regionalism undertaken on behalf of the Acton Society Trust—1 'Regional Institutions: a guide'; 2. 'Regionalism in England'; and 3. 'The New Regional Machinery'—are important contributions to the literature.

F. M. Blau and W. R. Scott undertake an interesting comparative study in *Formal Organisations*, Routledge & Kegan Paul, 1963, in which the concept of prime beneficiary is used. The student who is interested in the process of administration in the social services will find D. V. Donnison and Valerie Chapman's *Social Policy and Administration*, Allen & Unwin, 1965, well worth detailed attention as the series of case studies recorded there is unique.

The problems of professional people in organisations are touched upon in Roy Lewis and Angus Maude, *Professional People*, Phoenix House, 1952, and discussed in great detail in papers by a variety of writers collected in *Professionalization*, Prentice-Hall, New York, 1966, edited by H. M. Vollmer and Donald L. Mills. H. A. Simon's *Administrative Behaviour*, Collier-Macmillan, New York, 1957, is an important contribution to the literature about administration.

The report of the Committee on the Management of Local Government, 1967 (H.M.S.O.) discusses a number of interesting points and makes recommendations for the future which may have far-reaching results on the implementation of social policy.

The Report of the Committee on Local Authority and Allied Personal Social Services, Cmnd. 3703 (the Seebohm Report) and the Government's Green Paper on the Reorganisation of the National Health Service were both issued in July 1968 and will inevitably have important repercussions on the future organisation and administration of the social services. Apart from the discussion and recommendations in the main text of the Seebohm Report, the Appendices contain much valuable information for the student.

For a discussion of financial and manpower resources in Britain the H.M.S.O. publication, Cmnd. 2764, *The National Plan, 1965*, is essential even though some of its estimates have been overtaken by events. The Annual Reports of the different Ministries are also important for the student to consult.

This brief list can be extended indefinitely; the books to which reference is made in the text should be read in full by the serious student of social policy.

Bibliography

BLAU, P. M. and SCOTT, W. R. (1963), *Formal Organisations*, Routledge & Kegan Paul.

CARTWRIGHT, ANN (1964), *Human Relations and Hospital Care*, Routledge & Kegan Paul.

DONNISON, D. V. (1967), *The Government of Housing*, Penguin Books Ltd.

DONNISON, D. V., CHAPMAN, VALERIE and others (1965), *Social Policy and Administration*, Allen & Unwin.

FLETCHER, R. (1965), *Human Needs and the Social Order*, Michael Joseph.

GINSBERG, MORRIS (1965), *On Justice in Society*, Heinemann.

GOFFMAN, ERVING (1962), *Asylums: essays on the social situation of mental patients and other inmates*, Chicago: Aldine Press.

GRUSKY, OSCAR (1959), 'Role Conflict in Organisation', *Administrative Scene Quarterly*, 1959.

INSTITUTE OF ECONOMIC AFFAIRS (1965), *Choice in Welfare*.

KEITH-LUCAS, ALAN (1957), *Decisions about People in Need*, Oxford University Press.

MACKENZIE, W. J. M. and GROVE, JACK W. (1957), *Central Administration in Britain*, Longmans.

MARSHALL, T. H. (1963), *Sociology at the Crossroads and other essays*, Heinemann.

NATIONAL INSTITUTE FOR SOCIAL WORK TRAINING (1967), *Caring for People*.

PAIGE, DEBORAH and JONES, KIT (1966), *Health and Welfare Services in Britain in 1975*, Cambridge University Press for The National Institute of Economic and Social Research.

ROBERTS, DAVID (1960), *Victorian Origins of the British Welfare State*, Yale University Press.

BIBLIOGRAPHY

ROOFF, MADELINE (1957), *Voluntary Societies and Social Policy*, Routledge & Kegan Paul.

SELDON, ARTHUR (1966), in the *Social Service Quarterly*, Autumn 1966, in reply to a critical review of *Choice in Welfare* by D. C. Marsh.

SILBURN, R. L. (1965), 'Social Policy in Relation to Industrial Conditions', in *An Introduction to the Study of Social Administration*, ed. D. C. Marsh, Routledge & Kegan Paul.

SIMON, H. A. (1957), *Administrative Behaviour*, New York : Collier-Macmillan.

SLACK, KATHLEEN M. (1966), *Social Administration and the Citizen*, Michael Joseph.

SOUTH, BRIAN (1964), *Regionalism in England*, Vol. 1, Acton Society Trust.

STEVENS, ROSEMARY (1966), *Medical Practice in England*. Yale University Press.

TITMUSS, R. M. (1950), *Problems of Social Policy*, Longmans.

TITMUSS, R. M. (1958), *Essays on The Welfare State*, Allen & Unwin.

WADE, H. W. R. (1961), *Administrative Law*, Oxford University Press.